India Made Me
Britain Enabled Me

An Autobiography

India Made Me
Britain Enabled Me
An Autobiography

Dame Asha Khemka DBE DL

YATRA
BOOKS
An imprint of Vani Prakashan Group

vaniprakashan.com

Hardback First Edition : 2024

Yatra Books is an imprint of Vani Prakashan Group

Head Office

4695, 21-A, Daryaganj, New Delhi-110 002, India
Phone : +91 11 23273167, 11 23275710

Registered Bookstores and Offices

Ashok Rajpath, Patna-800 004, Bihar
Coffee House Campus, Mahatma Gandhi Marg, Allahabad-211 001, Uttar Pradesh
Mahatma Gandhi International Hindi University, Wardha-442 001, Maharashtra
36-A, Shakespeare Sarani, Near Rani Birla Girls College, Kolkata-700017, West Bengal

sales@vaniprakashan.in
vaniprakashan@gmail.com

India Made Me, Britain Enabled Me
An Autobiography
by Dame Asha Khemka DBE DL

ISBN : 978-93-5775-362-3
Autobiography

Printed and bound in India at Merohills Enterprise Pvt. Ltd.

India Made Me
Britain Enabled Me
An Autobiography

Dame Asha Khemka DBE DL

"I dedicate this book to my grandchildren Allegra and Xander.
I hope they will enjoy reading our story one day and learn a little more about their Maa and Dada"

Table of Contents

THE LORD BILIMORIA, CBE, DL

HOUSE OF LORDS
LONDON
SW1A 0PW

Foreword by Lord Karan Bilimoria

I have been privileged to know Dame Asha Khemka well for many years. Asha is someone who makes an impact wherever she goes and in whatever she does. From the time I first met her, I was inspired by her. And the more I learned about her, the more inspired I became. Her story is what dreams are made of; she is the living personification of the British dream. A child bride with three children, she followed her husband to the UK in her mid-20s, not speaking a word of English, rising to become a multiple award-winning leader of her profession in the UK – respected not just in this country but worldwide.

Asha has been the driving force behind championing the power of further education to transform young people's lives. I have seen first-hand the amazing work at the institution she headed as principal. There was an atmosphere of action, purpose and a can-do spirit, which all came from the top – from the principal – Asha Khemka.

She has been a powerful and fearless leader, fighting the cause not only of her institution but of her sector on the national stage. The proof of the pudding is in the eating, and she was listened to not just by the education sector but by the Prime Minister himself. Asha has been a role model to so many – to British Indians but also to the whole of the UK. People have looked up to her and been inspired by her. Her success has come from sacrifice, dedication, hard work and a clear sense of purpose, and her spirit has been infectious, enabling her to excel against all odds. As importantly, Asha has been devoted to her family – to her husband Shankar, a hugely accomplished surgeon – and her children Shalini, Sheel and Sneh. Asha's loyalty has not just been to her institution and her family but also to her friends, of which I am proud to count myself as one, to whom she shows unstinting loyalty and is a constant supporter.

The country of her birth India, has taken huge pride in this amazing daughter of India, a stellar star shining amongst the 30 million Indian diaspora around the world who have one by one been reaching the very top of their professions globally; Asha Khemka is an exemplar of this phenomenon.

This book will, I know, inspire so many, particularly young people in the UK and India, to aspire and achieve against all odds with integrity.

Karan

Lord Karan Bilimoria CBE DL

Member of the House of Lords
President of The CBI (Confederation of British Industry)
Chancellor of The University of Birmingham
Founder and Chairman of Cobra Beer

Preface
by
Darryl Eales

'Depth of Friendship does not depend on length of acquaintance'

Rabindranath Tagore

In these times of hyperbole and exaggeration, where fact and opinion are too often juxtaposed, there are thankfully some certainties.

This book IS joyous and uplifting. It WILL inspire and motivate. It IS a celebration of a remarkable woman who has lived an extraordinary life.

I vividly remember meeting Dame Asha for the first time. Elegant, immaculate, somewhat regal and, I have to admit, slightly scary!

We seamlessly hit it off. Asha's intensity and vitality shone through alongside an almost spiritual assuredness.

Rarely do you meet someone who has an immediate and profound impact on your life. In Asha's precise, considered and wonderfully articulate use of the English language, she pointed at my chest and said,

"Darryl, education is the silver bullet. It is the only thing that can change the destiny of a family in one generation."

Since then, some 14 years ago, our paths have been umbilically linked, through good times and those more challenging, blossoming to an ever-deeper friendship and an unbreakable bond of trust, loyalty and respect - all core principles ingrained in Asha's heart.

First and last, Asha is a devoted wife, wonderful mother and, latterly, proud grandmother with a deep love of family.

Since arriving in the UK some 45 years ago, she has embarked on her own journey of self-discovery whilst dedicating her life to young people and inspiring and encouraging them to be the best they can be.

I have visited West Nottinghamshire College regularly whilst Dame Asha was Principal and Chief Executive. The transformation and rebuilding of the College is a shining demonstration of how the vision and will of one person can change the destiny of a community and is the centrepiece of Asha's educational journey.

Visiting the College was always a pleasure and I was privileged to give the graduation address in 2017. The sense of joy and achievement was heart-warming and the deep respect and esteem for Dame Asha was clearly evident, from students, staff and parents alike.

Asha was always especially proud of the 'Inspire and Achieve Foundation' which provides support and nurturing for underprivileged youngsters and has turned around so many young lives.

She is equally at home with young people and parents or with statesmen or royalty. But she is always her authentic self.

She has very high standards and expectations. Family and closer friends will always remember being on the occasional receiving end of her disapprobation.

She most definitely does not suffer fools, is an active listener and is never short of offering an opinion. Work ethic is the universal foundation and she has little truck with empty words. As Abraham Lincoln said she absolutely served with "malice towards no-one and charity for all".

Her achievements and accomplishments are dwarfed by Asha the person. She really does have a joy and spirit for life - and a sense of humour to match - which enriches everyone she meets.

I have enjoyed many social occasions and family celebrations at the Khemka's magnificent family home in rural Staffordshire. This is Asha at her happiest and most relaxed surrounded by her close family and friends.

Shankar is her rock. An eminent orthopaedic surgeon in his own right, his unfailing support and gentle wisdom are ever present, always understated and always in the background.

Asha is a wonderful hostess. Guests are greeted with traditional Indian hospitality and made to feel as a much-loved family member.

And she knows how to party with a penchant for fine red wine, loves her music and is no mean dancer!

I fondly recall 'gate-crashing' Asha and Shankar's 40th wedding anniversary celebration in Delhi and being welcomed as family. I was captivated by meeting Devi Prasad Agrawal, her uncle who regaled a lifetime of stories about the rugged North of India and a window on the young Asha!

It has not always been a smooth path, even recently, and the Khemka family have experienced their fair share of the misfortunes, disappointments and unfairness that life throws at all of us.

I've learnt that you never really get to know your true self or the strength of your relationships until they have been tested by adversity.

This is when Asha is at her best - she is indefatigable, with a resilience and indomitable spirit which burns as brightly as ever today.

Tenacity, determination, cast iron will allied to a deep compassion for others and their struggles, even during her darker times.

And, of course, whatever the circumstances or situation, a passionate discussion about education and especially the debilitating impact of fear and poverty of hope has on the lives of too many people - and there is still much more to do.

Too often we forget to properly recognise or appreciate those who have helped, guided and supported us in our own lives.

I'm reminded of a favourite quote from Sir Isaac Newton, a man to whom we all owe so much;

"If I have seen further, it is by standing on the shoulders of giants"

Dame Asha - you are most certainly one such giant for so many and we are eternally grateful.

Darryl Eales

Chairman, E2Exchange
Chairman, Debrett's
Chairman, Solihull Moors Football Club
Chairman WERQWISE

Introduction

On the wall of my office at West Nottinghamshire College, I always looked to a plaque inscribed with the words of former US president Abraham Lincoln: 'Determine that the things can and shall be done, and then we shall find the way'. For 12 years, during my time as principal and CEO at the college, it was my firm belief that I, my colleagues, staff and students should strive to live by these words, and I often shared the quote with them.

This is a practice I have tried to adopt in my day-to-day life, but my journey has not been straightforward. I was born in the northern Indian state of Bihar. I was married at 15 to my husband, Shankar, and I embarked on the life of a wife and mother. But in 1978, my journey changed dramatically. When Shankar, a trainee surgeon, came to England to work and study, I followed closely behind with our three children Shalini, Sheel and Sneh.

At the time I left my homeland, I was 25 years old. Although I had matriculated from high school before my marriage, I had no further formal qualifications nor had I ever worked. Yet, my upbringing and loving family gave me the self-belief and confidence to take opportunities where I found them. In England, after my children had begun their own educational journeys, I embarked on mine.

I spoke no English, but I learned the basics of the language as my children learned it. When they were in boarding school, I took a typing course at a local college. From there, I got a job and worked my way up through the ranks from teacher to lecturer until I started the leadership role of my life in 2006. At West Nottinghamshire College, I became one of the first Asian principals and CEOs of a further education college in the UK. I have since been honoured as a Dame Commander of the Order of the British Empire, a Deputy Lieutenant of Staffordshire, and I have been fortunate enough to receive many accolades along the way. Mine was an unconventional educational route, but with determination I succeeded. Yet, my lifelong path of learning is not over. Every day is a day of discovery. Growing and developing myself further, challenging myself and challenging those around me to be better and to do better is my passion.

Not long after I became principal, I began to pass on my story of leadership and success to the students who entered through my college doors. Many came from complicated backgrounds in areas of high deprivation and low aspiration. I wanted to show them that if I could succeed, then there was nothing to stop them. They should never allow themselves to be held back from achieving their full potential. Through nurturing them and telling them they could reach the stars, I watched as many, embarked on careers they never thought possible. It is my firm belief that further education can unlock people's lives and change the destiny of a family in one generation.

The more I spoke about my own life, the more people told me I should write my story down: the journey from child bride to Dame. Starting from a position of no education, no knowledge and no exposure to the outside world taught me that regardless of which obstacles are in the way, they can be overcome. If I can inspire one person to achieve their dream, then I know I will have made a difference.

1

India Made Me

'A happy childhood is perhaps the most fortunate gift in life'

Dorothy Richardson

From a young age, I stood out from the crowd. I was self-assured and different to other girls in my home town of Sitamarhi, a town nestled on the border of northern India and Nepal. In the mornings, when I stepped outside of our family home, I attracted an audience. As the school bus pulled up opposite me on the dusty street, I remember the dozen-or-so girls on board rushing to gaze out of the open window.

'Look! Look at that girl! She is Vyjayanthimala,' they pointed at me excitedly as their eyes widened and their faces pressed against the glass.

A smile beamed across my face, and my heart swelled. Being compared to Vyjayanthimala made me feel very special. She was the first superstar actress of Indian Bollywood cinema, revered for her poise, grace and beauty. With almond eyes, plump lips and ebony hair, she radiated an inner joy and happiness. To think that I resembled her gave me a natural confidence that helped carry me in my young life, and it still does to this day.

Of course, I also have my family to thank for giving me such a sense of inner assurance. My father's family, the Agrawals, were not materially wealthy as such, but as a member of the Vaishya caste, I was born into India's business community. I was fortunate enough to grow up aware of poverty rather than it being my direct experience. Yet, my home state of Bihar was well known for being poor and lawless, as it still is to this day.

In 1951, the year of my birth, Bihar was beset by widespread famine and flooding. Across its sprawling, flat and mainly rural landscape, life was hard for many people, but our standard of living was high in comparison to others. We had no electricity but neither did anyone. Instead, our rooms would be lit with large gas lamps burning with kerosene oil.

While my upbringing was practical, down-to-earth and not luxurious, we ate well, dressed well and conducted ourselves with manners and an etiquette that stood out in the wider community.

Other families ate rice and vegetables, but my family served up toast and honey for breakfast. A tailor would come to the house, and I would instruct him on the precise way that I would like to be dressed and the design of each outfit – never the traditional saris that other girls and women wore. Instead, I designed pretty frocks that would not have looked out of place in England. In that sense, mine was a more westernised household, even though my family had never travelled outside of India. Certainly, I had never left Bihar and could not speak a word of English until after I arrived in the UK in the late 1970s.

When I was in my early teens, I recall an aunt of the same age who had attended an elite boarding school asking me, 'Asha, where do you get your etiquette from?' We were in a restaurant at the time, and she must have noticed how I pulled my shoulders back, sat up straight at the table and the way I held my knife and fork.

'Nowhere,' I replied, probably rather bluntly.

She seemed a little surprised. As I had grown up in rural India, I was certainly being viewed as backward rather than emanating style and confidence. But even today, I do not believe that anybody should be restrained by their upbringing. Life is about the belief you have in yourself, the opportunities given to you and whether you choose to take them rather than where society has pigeonholed you.

Exactly where my family etiquette came from, though, I am also unsure. Being a more educated family, I imagine that my parents and our extended family would have had more exposure to the British Raj, whose last viceroy left India four years before my birth. By the time I was born, Mahatma Gandhi had been assassinated and the bloody partition had divided British India into India and Pakistan. India was taking its first steps on its journey of independence. Nevertheless, the legacy of colonialism remained.

Although I was too young to remember the atmosphere in the country, I believe that people looked towards a new destiny with much hope but also apprehension. Nobody knew what effect the end of the British Empire would have on India or how the country would shape itself in the coming decades. It had the ambition, drive and intellectual capacity to have an impact on the world stage, but it would take many years for that to be realised. Having lived through Brexit in the UK, I suspect there was a similar feeling of loss, hope and the trepidation of stepping into the unknown.

Certainly, the ripple effects of partition were still being felt. Because we lived in a Hindu area, when I was around six years old, we were often targeted by Muslim agitators. These were people with whom we had lived side by side relatively peaceably, but now tension filled the air, and communal violence spilled over into the streets. Probably on the borders near Amritsar, this would have been felt more acutely, and certainly for us it became a more frequent occurrence.

'Come, you must hide,' my grandmother would say if ever the family knew that a mob was gathering outside and could storm the house. It was not uncommon to hear loud banging on the door and for the household to be catapulted into a state of panic. At the back of the house was a cowshed where we kept bullocks and buffalos. My brothers and I would be led to the haystacks there, and we huddled between them until the danger subsided, waiting anxiously for an elder to arrive to signal that calm had been restored.

My father, Ram Chandra Agrawal, was a tall, handsome man with a kind and generous nature but whose work in the construction industry took him away from home for long periods. Because of this, my formative years spent in Sitamarhi were mainly with my mother, grandmother, an aunt and several uncles. Then, there were my three brothers: Umesh, three years older than me; Suresh, who arrived one year after my birth; and my youngest brother, Dinesh, born the following year.

Now, when I think about Sitamarhi, I consider growing up there as one of the best times of my life. Outside, the streets bustled with cows, horses and bicycles carrying passengers and goods while the roadsides were lined with shops and market sellers. Worshippers drifted in and out of its temples carrying flowers, water or food as offerings to the gods.

The town itself is a very holy place and a pilgrimage site, central to versions of the Indian epic the *Ramayana*. According to the story, Sita, an incarnation of the goddess Lakshmi, is said to have been discovered in a clay pot in a furrow in a ploughed field in Sitamarhi. Soon after she was found, she was adopted and raised by Janak, King of Mithila, and his wife Sunaina and is closely associated with harvest and fertility.

Although my own family were not overly religious, I was brought up as a practising Hindu, and I would attend the temple every week. My grandmother also had a room at home where she kept a shrine. There, garlands of flowers hung, and the deep and woody smell of incense drifted from the shavings she burned from a sandalwood plate. A minty smell wafted from the sacred tulsi plants dotted around the room. Every morning at dawn, we would accompany her for our daily puja, lighting the pots that were filled with cotton wool and soaked in ghee, reciting our prayers to show humility and gratitude to our deities.

I myself was born on the first night of the Indian festival of Diwali, otherwise known as the festival of lights, which in that year of 1951 was the 21st October. Just before the arrival of the full moon, the streets would have been lit with brightly burning clay lamps while households celebrated the triumph of light over darkness, knowledge over ignorance and good over evil with family gatherings and sweets.

Today, wherever I am, I pray every morning and evening to the elephant god Ganesh, who represents prosperity, fortune and success. I also pray to the monkey god Hanuman, the *Ramayana*'s own superhero, who is associated with wisdom, strength, courage, devotion and self-discipline.

In Sitamarhi, I remember with such fondness our two-storey home built around a small courtyard. Every room was busy with the ebb and flow of people coming and going. There was always someone to come home to, and while the adults spent time on the verandas talking, I hopped from rooftop to rooftop high above the town playing with my brothers and my friends from the surrounding neighbourhood, in particular my friend Sharda Poddar with whom I have kept a lifelong bond.

I also played in our large kitchen while the servants worked and the cook prepared food. The sounds, smells and tastes were overwhelming as vegetables were chopped, pots boiled on the stove and bread baked in the oven. To this day,

I have a vision of myself running home from school and perching on a pile of wood stacked up high on the side of our large clay cooker, swinging my legs as I relayed stories about my day to my aunt who listened patiently. No matter how blazing hot the oven temperature became, I stayed sitting in the same spot to talk with her.

Now, when I think about it, I can still taste the deliciousness of my favourite dishes, prepared with love. As a young girl, I had such a sweet tooth, and wherever I went, sweet treats would be offered to me. My uncle even bought an electric oven to bake a cake – a novelty at the time in our community. After dinner, we would be served tasty puddings with his own hand-prepared custard. At the house of my friend Bimla, I would eat paneer, fashioned into tiny grains like rice with butter and served with saffron and sugar syrup, cardamom, almonds and cashews. I have never found this dish anywhere else yet the thought of it immediately transports me back to Bihar and my childhood.

Growing up in a multi-generational household gave me a feeling of security and a sense of belongingness and protection that also stood me in good stead for the many challenges ahead in my life. But, as the first girl gifted to my family for three generations, there was also no doubt that I was placed on a pedestal. I was loved and nurtured by the elders around me, and I believe this also added to my sense of self.

Certainly, my grandmother spoiled me, and this was a well-known fact throughout our family. She always treated me differently to the other children. Perhaps it was because she had not had a daughter of her own, but she and I developed a naturally close bond – the same special bond I feel now with my own granddaughter, Allegra.

'Come, come, Asha,' my grandmother would say, tapping me on the shoulder and leading me to her room. There, she would place her finger to her lips to signal that what she was about to do was a secret to be kept between us. Inside her wardrobe, she kept jars of expensive nuts like cashews, almonds and pistachios. She carefully undid the lids, taking out a handful to place into my mouth away from the presence of my brothers.

My uncles also doted on me, and I consider myself very lucky to have been the focus of so much attention. One uncle, who studied across different towns throughout Bihar, always brought me back the best dresses from his travels: beautiful, Western-style frocks. One that sticks in my mind was pink with chiffon frills cascading down its bodice and sleeves.

If I wanted a new pair of shoes, my uncles would also not hesitate to buy them for me, even if they risked being told off for doing so.

On one memorable occasion, I travelled to Patna – Bihar's capital city – to my grandfather's home. While out shopping with one uncle, Bhagwati, I saw the most fashionable pair of shoes staring out at me from a store window.

'I like these so much, Chacha,' I said to him.

'If you like them Asha, then I will buy them for you,' he offered.

'Thank you, Chacha,' I said, thrilled at the present being bought.

The shoes were smart and made of leather, and it felt so special to slip my feet into them, but by the time I had tried them on, we had lost track of time and arrived home late for dinner. Normally, this would not have been a problem, but my grandfather was a strict man – a chief justice in Bihar state and a stickler for time. If dinner was served at 7 p.m., we were expected to be at the table, not a moment later.

'Bhagwati, where have you been today? Why are you so late?' my grandfather demanded to know.

'Asha and I went shopping, and I bought her a new pair of shoes,' my uncle replied hesitantly.

'How much were the shoes?' my grandfather continued to grill him.

The shoes were very expensive, and when my uncle revealed the price tag, he was treated to an outburst from my grandfather.

'How dare you! You must learn to live within your means,' he shouted. 'I would not buy these shoes even for my own daughter!'

This comment was so hurtful to my uncle, as my grandfather was a man of some stature. But I watched on as my uncle bravely fought my corner.

'You may not be able to afford these for your daughter, but I can afford to buy Asha anything I like,' he snapped before pulling his chair back and walking from the room. That night, I slipped out silently behind him, and he and I ate elsewhere. Secretly, I was pleased. I had my new pair of shoes, and my uncle had fought for me – there was no better feeling in the world.

At other times, my uncles would dress me up and take me to the market or to festivals and melas to show me off to their friends in the community. Whatever I wore soon became the fashion in Sitamarhi. I guess you could say I was an influencer from an early age. Sometimes, I was taken to be photographed in the local studio. I would spend hours there while the photographer arranged me in different poses. Even now, I have kept a photograph of myself aged only a few months old sitting beside my two Alsatians – a sight that would have been very unusual in rural India in the 1950s.

Just as I had a natural bond with my grandmother, I was also very close to my mother, Mohini, even though my last memories of her are of a woman in poor health. Doctors never fully understood what was wrong with her, but I was nearing the end of my primary education when she became ill with a suspected heart condition.

At around the same time, my father ended his work in the construction industry and set up a butter and ghee factory in Muzaffarpur, a city south of Sitamarhi where I was transferred to school. Although my father struggled to make the business a success, we stayed there for around a year.

Slowly, I noticed that my mother, who was a beautiful, fair-skinned and chubby woman, had started to become short of breath. The smoke in the kitchen in Muzaffarpur hung thick and heavy as the food was being prepared, and I saw how she coughed and wheezed and how her body tired more easily.

'We can't stay here. We can't continue to live like this,' I told my father one day. As a child of around 11 years old, I felt such deep emotional pain for my mother, whose condition I watched deteriorate over time. What was worse was the helplessness of knowing that nothing I could do could make her better. Perhaps for this reason, I felt more grown-up than other girls of my age – a person who naturally took on more responsibility.

Eventually, when my father's business failed, my parents relocated to Riga, a small village north of Sitamarhi where my father established a dairy farm with my uncle and aunt. Although the main house there was spacious and my brothers remained to attend school and work on the farm, I returned to Sitamarhi to live temporarily with my grandmother, who always fought for me to be with her.

There, I began my secondary school studies at Kamala Girls School. Other girls boarded at the high school, but as my family lived nearby, I travelled there each day. Every morning, I would leave home dressed in my sky-blue kurta and white salwar and walk through the school grounds, always stopping to notice the beautiful yellow flowers, roses and the butterflies moving from flower to flower gathering pollen.

Growing up, I suppose I never saw education as a privilege. It was something that all girls of my background did, even if they would go on to become wives and mothers and would never enjoy a career after they matriculated. Although the servants in our house and their children would not have attended school, it is maybe only later in life that I feel gratitude for my head-start. At the time, literacy rates in Bihar were very low, especially for girls. Even now, around a third of Bihar's total population remains illiterate, and more than half of these are girls.

In class, I was good at studying. I was disciplined and did everything that was expected of me – not a genius by any means but intellectually average and someone who never got into trouble. That I would make my way through school and matriculate was an accepted fact in our family. In this way, I was not treated any differently to my brothers. In fact, perhaps unusually as a girl growing up in India, I was encouraged by my grandmother to be independent and speak my own mind.

If there were times when my youngest uncle, Ram Sharan, asked me to fetch him a glass of water from the kitchen, I would simply reply, 'No. Go and get it yourself'. Likewise, if I was taken to a relative's house, perhaps for a religious gathering, and I refused to join in with the dancing and singing, nobody ever forced me to. I was known to be headstrong risking being told off but, often with my grandmother's support, I got away with being rebellious.

Mostly though, I went with the flow of what was expected of me. For example, all girls knew that a time would come when their marriage would be arranged. As it was for my mother, my life would be planned out for me according to the rituals and principles of our society. If I had stayed in Bihar, it is unlikely I ever would have learned English or come to experience a life outside of being a wife and mother. Back then, these things were never analysed or questioned.

Looking back, I wish I had challenged this status quo more and displayed more of a leadership role, even as a teenager. For instance, when I think now about the lonely days spent isolating on the second floor of our house in

Sitamarhi during menstruation, as was the tradition for women, I wonder, *How did I allow that to happen? Why did I not try to change something*? Instead, I accepted it as part of life. Likewise, I accepted the inevitability of an arranged marriage. Of course, hindsight is a wonderful thing.

As the only girl in the family, I was also called upon to look after my mother when her health deteriorated further. Alongside the servants and the chef in Riga, I was brought from Sitamarhi to assist with her care, even if this meant being removed from school. At the age of 12, my studies at Kamala Girls School ended abruptly. Again, I do not remember ever being resistant to this, and while I missed my lessons and my friends, I came back to see them regularly. For me, it was my unquestionable duty to be with my mother.

At first, adjusting to this new way of life was hard, but I did it willingly. My mother was mainly bedridden by now, and each day was spent washing her, helping her dress, massaging her to ease her breathing, making sure she took her medicine on time, that she was fed properly and at the same time making sure my younger brothers were also dressed and in school on time.

Sometimes, I would get up early to ride my horse across the misty fields around the farm, dressed in my cap and tweed jacket and clutching my stick – another stylish outfit bought for me by my uncles. On other mornings, I helped to milk the cows as I watched the sun rise before I began my daily routine.

As I spent time with my mother, we developed an even closer bond. Sadly, I recall little about her other than her striking beauty and that she was pristine. In fact, my daughter Shalini reminds me very much of her in looks, even down to her tiny feet. Every evening, my mother would take a shower and dress in her most beautiful sari and spray perfume on herself before dinner, regardless of whether my father was there or not, which was unusual for a woman. Even when she was ill, she made every effort to get up and get dressed.

On the first day of my periods, she sat me down and talked to me woman to woman for the first time, and I sensed in her a gentleness and care, even though she was struggling so badly with her own health.

'Don't worry about me, Asha. I am fine,' she always said, downplaying the severity of her condition so that the burden of responsibility would not weigh heavily on me. I remember her kindness. Anything I wanted would be prepared for me in the kitchen, especially balushahi – the Indian equivalent to doughnuts but with a crispy shell – which I loved to eat.

It must have been around six months after arriving in Riga when I was in the back garden walking among the mango trees laden with ripe fruit and the flowering lychee trees. The day is so memorable because my grandmother had come from Sitamarhi to visit. In a small room in the house furnished with sofas and sandalwood curtains, we sat and had tea, and it was just before lunch that my mother asked me to collect some food from the garden so it could be prepared.

I had picked a spicy vegetable for her, and I was just about to return to the house when the air was pierced with a long chilling scream.

'Maa?' My body froze momentarily, and a silence descended over the garden. I dropped everything and ran inside.

In her room, my mother lay on the bed.

'Maa?' I screamed over and over, but her chest was still, and her eyes were closed. By now, the whole family had rushed to my mother's bedside, and I was led away, sobbing uncontrollably. There was no time to say goodbye. On the day my mother died, she was only 33 years old.

In the months that followed my mother's death, I was devastated. As was our tradition, girls did not attend a mother's funeral, but I mourned her passing with many tears. Her body was taken soon after her death to the nearby river where she was cremated. Despite being supported by family, as I had always been, the rooms in the house in Riga felt emptier. My heart longed to see my mother again and to feel her care and closeness. I was not a person who spoke openly about this, not even to my grandmother. I kept my grief inside and got on with life.

For my brothers, there was a vacuum of love that needed to be filled, and I stepped in to help care for them both practically and emotionally. It would be me who Suresh and Dinesh would turn to if they ever had a problem or needed to talk, and I would advise them as best I could.

Now, I wonder how I overcame this challenging period and coped with what was about to follow. After around a year, my father remarried. He was in his 40s, young enough to begin a new life with someone else, but for us – especially my older brother Umesh and me – our mother was irreplaceable.

'Why is this happening to us?' we often asked. All we saw was the unfairness of the situation, and we struggled with the readjustment.

Perhaps life would have been easier had my father's second wife been a person we naturally warmed to. Sadly, there was no bond and very little affection between us. When she tried to take charge of my younger brothers, I instinctively lashed out.

'You will eat what you are given,' I overheard her say to Suresh and Dinesh one day. Immediately, I felt anger prickle on my skin.

'Get lost. Never speak to my brothers like that again,' I said, staring her down until she backed away.

From that moment onwards, my stepmother took a back seat. She could sense how forceful and determined I could be and how protective of my brothers I was. If a person did not show them respect, I would always step in. With time, she and I found an equilibrium, but it was one based on a mutual tolerance of each other rather than any deep love.

Soon, I was back with my grandmother in Sitamarhi. There, I resumed my schooling at Kamala Girls School, where I threw myself into my studies and various leadership roles. I graduated to head girl and also became an active recruit in the National Cadet Corps – the youth wing of the Indian Armed Forces, where I wore my cap and khaki uniform with pride.

In many ways, those early school years prepared me for the career I pursued later on in life. I leaned in naturally to the order of regimentation even if at home, I sometimes resisted being told what to do. As an NCC cadet, I would be expected to hold a rifle and march with my group for local parades and also take part in the large parades to celebrate India's Independence Day on 15th August and Republic Day on 26th January.

At school, I had first become a monitor in Chapman Girls' High School during the year when I accompanied my parents to Muzaffarpur. When this continued at Kamala Girls' School, I loved the feeling of responsibility and power that the role gave me. Admittedly, I also loved to wear a smart uniform. It transformed me and made me feel invincible.

It was not until many, many years later, in 2018, that I returned to Kamala Girls' School. I had been with my husband Shankar visiting family in Sitamarhi, when we were passing by one evening accompanied by my uncle, Ram Sharan. I creaked open the steel doors and wandered around the grounds. The paint was peeling on the walls, and the building looked neglected compared to when I was a student there. As I walked, I pictured myself as a young girl on her hands and knees spreading the cow-dung paste over the school floor to clean it or sitting at my small wooden desk, wide-eyed and eager to learn. My thoughts were interrupted by a man who came out to greet us.

'Can I help you?' he said, introducing himself as the gatekeeper.

'I'm Asha Khemka. I was once a pupil here,' I told him, but he had already recognised me and knew my family in Sitamarhi. The very next day, the headmaster rang my uncle and asked if I would come to speak to the girls studying there to inspire them and pass on my story of success.

I was filled with excitement, but admittedly, I was also a little anxious. In the hall, I looked out onto around 3,000 students.

'Would you like me to speak in English or Hindi?' I asked the girls.

The girls wanted me to speak in Hindi, which by then I was unaccustomed to, but I got through it. As I looked into their eyes, I saw myself at their age. I told them to aim high, that they could be anything they wanted to be with dedication and determination. I was overwhelmed by the reception given to me by the students, the teachers and the headmaster. I was also pleasantly surprised when one of the retired administrators from my time at the school came to see me and showed me the records of my admission to the school. Yet, my heart felt heavy, too. I came away from the school saddened at how run-down it had become. Immediately, I thought, *How can I change this? How can I make it better*? This is a fundraising plan I am still working on.

For me, it was also to be a long road to success. Within two years of my mother's death, my burgeoning sense of independence was to be unexpectedly taken from me. My life was about to change again, forever.

My first photograph with my two Alsatian bodyguards in Sitamarhi

Me with my three brothers Umesh, Suresh and Dinesh at our home in Riga

Me sitting on the veranda age 12 at our Riga home

In my captain's NCC (National Cadet Corps) uniform, age 14

My loving grandmother, Srimati Anari Devi

My beloved father,
Mr Ramchandra Agrawal

My darling mother,
Mrs Mohini Agrawal

My first photo wearing a sari

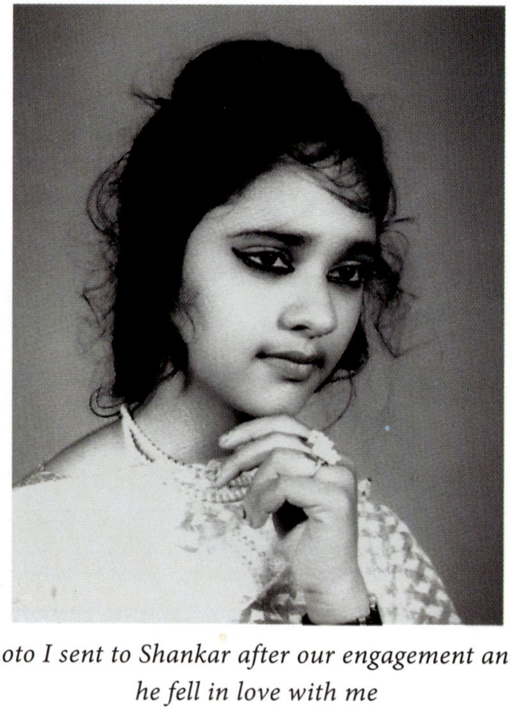

The first photo I sent to Shankar after our engagement and apparently he fell in love with me

One of my favourite photos of my youth

One of Shankar's favourite photos which he took during our first holiday in Ranchi, four years after we got married

2

The Struggle Within

'If you cry because the sun has gone out of your life, your tears will prevent you from seeing the stars'

Rabindranath Tagore

'Come, Asha. I am going to put this sari on you,' my aunt said to me one day while I was at her house in Bettiah during the school holidays. We were in her bedroom, and I thought the instruction was strange. I had never dressed in a sari before.

'Why?' I asked, full of curiosity.

'There are people coming to see you today'.

'Coming to see me for what?' I was confused.

'For your marriage proposal,' she said matter-of-factly.

My marriage proposal? My body tensed, and panic overwhelmed me.

Although I knew my marriage would be arranged one day, I had not expected it to come out of the blue as it did. I had not long turned 14 years old, and I had not yet matriculated from high school. Besides, until that day, I had no clue who my proposed husband even was.

When my father came to see me, he sat me down.

'This young man is very handsome. He is a medical student, and we approve of him,' he explained, but I was barely listening to his words.

All I could think about was how sudden all of this was and how little control I had over events. Unexpectedly, I had already lost my mother. Although I did not show it to the outside world, my sense of loss was immense. Now, I had another adjustment in my life to cope with and another set of responsibilities to assume.

Tears rolled down my cheeks. 'What is this? Why are you doing this to me?' I cried, but my upset fell on deaf ears.

My aunt had stitched her own blouse on me so it fitted my girlish frame. Just as she finished plaiting my hair, pleating my skirt and draping the pallu of my sari around my shoulder, I heard footsteps in the hallway. A coach-load of my husband-to-be's family had arrived. His parents came along with his brothers and sister. Even his friends came and filled the living room of my aunt's house.

Unbeknownst to me, Shankar's sister-in-law had been planning a match between us behind the scenes for some months, and even though we had never met, our families were already closely entwined. Before settling in Bihar, my family had originated from Untwal in Rajasthan, the central Indian state that was the jewel in the crown of the Mughal Empire. Shankar's family also originated from the same area, which was known for its exquisite palaces, havelis and mountain forts. His family knew my family, and the two families had some common friends and relations. Both families spoke the Rajasthani language called Marwari, so our societal and cultural bond was deep.

Before that day, my father had already visited Shankar's father in Motihari, the town where his family lived. Shankar himself had been driven to my grandfather's house in Patna, where they had both been introduced and the marriage agreed upon. 'If you marry into Asha's family, it will bring seven generations of prosperity,' Shankar's father had told him. The only person that had not been consulted about it until that day had been me.

Even then, I did not meet my proposed husband. The only person missing on the day of my engagement was Shankar himself. He was studying for his pre-medical exams in Patna and had chosen not to take the day out from his classes. Apparently, he was already head-over-heels in love with me – or at least the idea of me – from the photographs he had seen and the many stories he had heard about me through his family and friends. Three or four other girls had been proposed to him, but he had rejected all of them.

Although he had seen pictures of me, I had never set eyes on Shankar. But that afternoon in June 1966, when his family came to my aunt's, my dad handed me a photograph of him. Immediately, my stomach tensed.

'Who is this old man?' I thought. He was handsome, but he looked far too old for me, even though Shankar was only around 18 at the time. Yet, I kept my feelings hidden. If this was the man my family had chosen for me to marry, then I went along with it. Of course, if I had said 'no,' another suitor would have been found. But I said 'yes,' despite feeling violated by the experience.

In my aunt's living room, I sat quietly with my head bowed while Shankar's family fussed around me. 'You are beautiful,' they said, but I was too confused to respond. How could this be happening to me like this? Within an hour, I had been decorated with gold earrings, bangles, necklaces and a headdress and told I was now engaged.

When the food was served and the party began, another surprise awaited me. When I took something to eat, I began to understand a little of how different Shankar's family were to mine. Naturally, I ate it in front of the guests as I would do in my own family. There, we had no special rules for girls, but Shankar's mother tapped me.

'In our family, you eat with your head turned so no one sees,' she whispered. I found this very difficult to hear. Shankar's family were far more traditional than my own, and in those initial stages, I wondered if my more liberal upbringing would be forgotten about and I would be expected to fall in line. It would be some time before I ever knew.

Shankar remained in Patna for a whole eight months after our engagement. During that time, he did not travel to see me, nor did I visit him. Instead, we sent letters every week. From the outset, we wrote six- or seven-page epics filled with all the romance of a burgeoning love affair. We told each other how we imagined each other, how we could not wait to spend our lives together. I pressed delicate rose petals and placed them between the pages. Neither of us contemplated that our marriage would never work; it was a cast-iron guarantee. We were made for each other, and we were in love. Besides, in India, a marriage is not between two individuals. It is a joining of two people, two families and two communities.

At the time, the Bollywood movie *Teesri Manzil* had been released, and I called Shankar 'Sona' in my letters after the film's love interest, played by the very dashing Bollywood star Shammi Kapoor. The heroine of the film was played by the actress Asha Parekh, so I became Shankar's very own Asha. After we married, we went to see that film together one evening.

When Shankar and I eventually did meet face to face, it was in the town of Bettiah. My father had moved there with us and his new wife and had begun a pharmacy business with a relative named Asha Pharmacy, after me. I will never forget that day. It could have been the most famous scene from the Shakespeare play *Romeo and Juliet,* played out on our own stage with as much longing and passion. I was standing on the first-floor balcony of the store, when I looked down to see Shankar walking on the road as part of the procession to celebrate the pharmacy's opening. He was exactly the fiancé I had imagined in my dreams: a handsome, dashing, well-dressed man who looked so romantic, charming and curious. He was looking up beyond the balcony, so I was able to study him for some time. Now, I know he was looking for me, excited to discover who I was for the first time.

The next day, we met in person. When Shankar came to our house, I was cooking. I noticed he was dressed to impress in new pilot-green trousers and a smart white shirt for the occasion. On the other hand, I was sitting on the veranda floor, rolling dough out for chapati, and we secretly stole a glance at each other.

Later, we met more formally but in the presence of my brother Suresh. As we were not married yet, there needed to be a chaperone present, but I have never forgotten the feeling of our first touch. While we were talking, Shankar reached his finger over and stroked the top of mine. Suddenly, it felt as though an electric current had surged through me. We were living in the moment, just enjoying falling in love, even though we would not see each other again until the day of our wedding ceremony.

The three-day ceremony itself took place in my aunt's house in Bettiah. Ever since my mother's death, she had supported me alongside my grandmother. Money had been tight for my father, and both women understood the difficult relationship I had with my stepmother. Being my mother's elder sister, my aunt was protective over me. She was generous and gave me whatever I needed for my wedding. My grandmother had also been saving for many years for the day I got married.

'Take whatever you need, Asha,' I remember my aunt saying to me. Looking back, I was so lucky to have that support. I could choose whatever sari or jewellery I wanted for the occasion, and in the weeks running up to our celebration, I spent many hours trying on jewellery and saris and having my wedding outfits adjusted to fit.

On the day the festivities began, I felt a nervous excitement, but this soon turned overwhelming at the magnitude of it all. I had seen other girls marry, and I had been to weddings, but nothing had prepared me for how I would feel. Around 200 people gathered in Bettiah from all over Bihar to celebrate. The procession drums beat out Shankar's arrival, and as I waited, I could hear the deafening sound of the band getting closer and closer. When Shankar finally entered my aunt's courtyard on a horse, my stepmother came forward to measure his chest – a wedding ritual designed to show how strong the groom is. When we stood together – me in a gold sari and Shankar in his suit – we exchanged flower garlands. I was so scared that I could barely look him in the eye.

The actual wedding ceremony did not start until well after midnight. Flowers decorated the trees around my aunt's courtyard, and a fire burned as I came to sit on the right-hand side of Shankar, as is our custom. Given the more traditional nature of his family, his sister had dressed me in a veil that reached my shoulders. I hated it. On the way to the ceremony, I could barely see my brother Suresh in front leading me to the courtyard. I felt shrouded in a veil of darkness, all the time wondering, 'How is this happening?'

As I sat beside Shankar, emotion welled up inside of me. The veil was not what I wanted, even though I knew it was what my father-in-law would have expected. Thankfully, my uncle Bhagwati sensed my discomfort, and not long after I sat down on the dais, he stood up in front of the crowd and approached me. Gently, he lifted my veil over my tikka so that my head remained covered but I could see. Immediately, a weight lifted from me. I felt relief to have it removed and also that Shankar's father did not object.

As we repeated our vows, we placed our hands over one another's, and on each of the seven promises we made to one another, we walked around the fire. At the ceremony's completion, I moved and stood on Shankar's left side to signify that I was now a married woman. By now, I was so tired I could barely stand up. The ceremony had lasted around four hours, and the whole occasion seemed like a blur. All I can picture now is the smoke from the fire filling the courtyard and the lines of well-wishers telling me how beautiful I was as the intensity of the atmosphere pulsed through me.

This continued the next day, but by then, I could not stop myself from breaking down in tears following our farewell from Bettiah. The wedding procession had travelled to Motihari, to Shankar's family home, where the party continued. However, I was filled with the sadness of knowing that it was the last time I would live with my family. I was almost existing on autopilot, just trying to cope with the immensity of it all. Again, I was expected to stand like a showpiece while the guests fussed over me.

My father-in-law had wanted the band to play a very famous Bollywood song called 'Baharon Phool Barsao Mera Mehboob Aya Hai,' which means 'Seasons of spring, shower with flowers, my beloved has come.' The song, sung for Vyjayanthimala in the film *Suraj*, played over and over as the procession led its way into Shankar's house. But just as I was following Shankar and we were poised to step over the threshold, the whole house was plunged into darkness. A power cut had struck, which only added to my sense of utter bewilderment. As was the tradition then, my face was also covered in a long veil. I had never seen Shankar's family home before, and I was exhausted. It felt like being led blindfolded into a strange and alien world.

During one ritual called Sirguthi, Shankar's sister took me into a side room to oil and plait my hair so I was refreshed for the hours ahead. As is also the custom, my face was covered again. As they placed the tikka in my hair, tears rolled down my cheeks. Mostly, I was struck by the lack of control I had over my own life and my own destiny, even though I was in love with Shankar, and I was sure it was him I wanted to marry.

In the days and weeks ahead, this feeling only intensified. Whereas it is usual for couples to consummate the marriage on their wedding night, this did not happen for me. I was so naive about anything to do with sex that I thought if Shankar even kissed me, I would get pregnant. Every time he approached, I would hide behind my mother-in-law.

'Go. Go now, Asha,' she would gently direct me towards him, but that uncertainty remained for a while until I could trust the situation. Thankfully, Shankar was not a forceful man and understood that I needed to be ready.

What was even more challenging for me was the new regime I now entered into after I moved to living full-time with Shankar's family. In Motihari, Shankar's parents and his two elder brothers, their wives and his four younger brothers all lived in a two-storey house. The standard of living was not what I had been used to. There were no servants, and the women worked so hard to do everything themselves. I watched as Shankar's mother rose at 4 a.m. to tend the cows before feeding the men and managing the household. A full meal would be prepared for them instead of breakfast, which they ate before work. Women in Shankar's house always ate afterwards.

There were also new expectations placed upon me, even though I was barely 15. For example, I would rise and go to the temple with the others – not a routine I was used to. However, what struck me the most was that the children in the house were treated differently. In our home, children were at the centre of everything. They were the first to be fed and looked after, but in Shankar's parents' house, children always came second. They were not mistreated in any way, but I observed this lack of attention compared to my own upbringing, and it troubled me.

From early on, I did raise this issue with my sister-in-law and my mother-in-law as it became so painful for me. 'Children are our future,' I said. 'They need more attention. They need proper nutrition and proper care,' I pleaded. Things did slowly start to change, more so when my sister-in-law gave birth to a baby girl and I offered to take charge and show her a different way of caring. She did not resist. Instead, she watched me feed, bathe and dress the baby, and she learned that way. I also started to teach the other children in the house in the hope that they would be better at their studies.

Although I had matriculated from high school before my marriage, there was no expectation for me to enter further education or ever work. My path as a wife and mother was mapped out for me the day I got engaged to Shankar. I was expected to get on with it. It is hard for me to remember exactly how I felt, but certainly being in a strange house with a family unlike mine took its toll. As the months went on, I lost a lot of weight. I used to starve myself regularly, perhaps as an attempt to regain control over my life.

'Asha, you look different. Why? What has happened?' family members asked me when I went back to Sitamarhi to visit. I did not know why. Maybe this was happening unconsciously.

What made it even worse was that Shankar and I did not live together for some time after our wedding. He remained in Patna to finish his medical training, and when he finally got his bachelor of medicine in 1970, he stayed on to embark on his first house officer's job.

For four years between our marriage in February 1967 and me leaving Motihari, we only saw each other four or five times a year. I longed to see him, and he felt the same. When he did come, Shankar would cross the Ganges by boat and then take the overnight train headed for home. For those few nights after his arrival, we hardly slept. We talked and talked and enjoyed each other's company, our love growing day by day.

One time, I had been called to go to Bettiah to my father's home, when Shankar arrived from Patna.

'Where is she? How could you let this happen? She is not here!' Shankar said to his mother angrily when he greeted her. He had been so excited to see me, yet our room was empty. Soon, my brother-in-law arrived to fetch me back to Motihari.

When we were together, we looked so glamorous that people stopped us in the street. 'You are so beautiful. Are you brother and sister?' they said. I would be in full makeup with a sari, and Shankar would also be dressed very smartly. We became a reflection of each other, hence the confusion that we were related. Or people would ask, 'Are you film stars?'

Our first holiday spent together is still imprinted in my mind. We travelled to Ranchi, now the capital city of Jharkhand state. There, the crystal-white waters of the Hundru Falls hit against the rocks, and for a while, we lost ourselves in the depths of the forests, the natural beauty of the landscape and our love for each other. Everything felt so intense that when we eventually parted, all we could think about was when we would see each other again. Emptiness overwhelmed us, and like so many times before, we parted with tears streaming down our faces.

On another occasion, I travelled to Patna to attend a family wedding. Although we were not supposed to be living with each other, a kind uncle let me slip out and board with Shankar at night in his hostel, so much was our longing to be together.

Eventually, when Shankar qualified as a doctor, I was able to join him in his rented accommodation in Patna. There, we embarked on another period of readjustment. It is hard for us to believe now, but we had so little money that we had to borrow from family members. We could not even afford a proper bed, and so we slept on a wooden chowki and a thin mattress.

Shankar was also jealous, which amuses me even today. If ever he was out and his friends came over, I would get the third degree afterwards.

‘Why did they come over? What did they say?’ he demanded to know, but the truth was I never had eyes for any of Shankar’s friends – only him. From the outset, I never questioned the trust we had between us.

At the time, we were not thinking about children, but when children did not happen straight away, Shankar’s mother became concerned. I have no memory of this, but Shankar recalls her taking me to an obstetrician in Motihari. I must have been around 18, and after I was examined, the obstetrician said I had an infantile uterus and that children may be hard for me.

I cannot think this had much of an impact because not long after I moved to Patna, I became pregnant with our daughter Shalini. By that time, my mother- and father-in-law were also living with us in our rented accommodation alongside Shankar’s brother, who was studying dentistry.

While I was delighted to be expecting, pregnancy was very hard for me. Not only was I sick around 20 times a day and the only thing I wanted to do was sleep, but I felt the presence of my in-laws in the house. I worried how I might be judged if I did not fulfil my household duties.

Money was also still tight for us. Shankar’s trainee doctor’s salary did not bring in that much each month, and so my grandmother kindly filled that gap by sending saris and jewellery for me and clothes for the new baby. She knew life was different for me now, and she did everything she could to cushion that impact. I also adjusted. If I only had four saris and four blouses, then so be it. I made the best of what I had.

On the night Shalini was born, I spent the whole day in labour. But the minute I held her in my arms, my whole world changed. All the attention I had given to myself in the run-up to being a mother transferred to her. As I held her tiny fingers and looked into her face, I felt an overwhelming urge to take care of her, even though Shalini turned out to be quite a challenging baby. Sleepless nights became a regular occurrence, and with Shankar working long hours – sometimes from 5 a.m. until 10 p.m. – it fell on me to get up in the night and feed her and be with her during the day.

Again, I started to lose weight and starve myself. People also commented that I was not the same person. ‘What is happening to you, Asha?’ they would ask. I was not as pristine in the way I had been before, simply because I did not have the time or the energy. Often, I did not like the way I looked, but I got on with raising Shalini in the way that I wanted to. Now, Shankar reflects on that period differently to how I felt at the time. Before marriage and children, he says he saw me as free, like a bird before it became caged. Perhaps all that was going on beneath the surface, but it was unconscious. I felt responsibility and duty rather than imprisonment. Besides, all the women around me were living this life. There was no route out.

Also impacting our family life was Shankar's father, who had become very sick and died suddenly after a short illness. It was a traumatic time for all of us, and to this day, Shankar wishes he had admitted his father to hospital earlier. Unnecessarily, he still blames himself for the death of his father, who had only been in his mid-50s when he passed away. In truth, nothing may have saved him. The most important thing was that we had time with him in Patna, and he met his granddaughter before he died.

After we took his body back to Motihari for his funeral, Shankar's mother also returned to the family home for good, and we returned to Patna alone. More children followed in quick succession. Sheel arrived around one and a half years after Shalini. A more placid baby by nature, I also loved nurturing him, but life was not without its drama.

Not long after Sheel was born, I was in the kitchen when I heard a loud cry and a thud. My heart almost stopped as I imagined what had happened. When I rushed through onto the veranda, Sheel was fast asleep in his cot, but Shalini was nowhere to be seen.

'Shalini?' I shouted. But the room was filled with an eerie silence. Desperately, I looked around before I made my way onto the balcony. One storey down, lying on the road below was Shalini's tiny body. When I rushed downstairs, my heart was pounding out of my chest. The moment I reached her, I could feel her breath on my hand, but her eyes were firmly closed as she lay there.

I had to think on my feet. There was a paediatrician who Shankar and I were friends with who lived nearby, and after I scooped Shalini up in my arms, I ran and ran.

'Please, God. Please be OK,' I repeated to myself with every step, and after I banged on the door for help, the paediatrician answered, confused by my panic.

'What's the matter, Asha? What has happened?' he asked. I barely had time to explain before I was bundled into the back of his car and driven to the hospital. Shalini's tiny chest was still rising and falling, but her eyes remained shut as they did for the next four days. Miraculously, when doctors examined her, she was not permanently injured but had suffered a hairline fracture on her skull. At the time of the accident, Shankar was working at another hospital and arrived at the A&E department as soon as the news got to him.

For that whole week, I travelled back and forth to the hospital. The wife of a surgeon friend of ours also came to the house to take care of Sheel and relieve me of the household duties. By now, the accident was the talk of the town, and while no one said anything to my face, I could not help feeling that people were gossiping and pointing a finger at me, judging me as a neglectful mother. In truth, I could not help thinking how Shalini's strength had surprised me. A table and chair had been placed on the veranda precisely to stop any child from falling, yet she had moved them to one side and stepped off. To this day, I cannot even imagine how close we were to losing her.

In fact, the accident did not seem to affect Shalini at all. She was already a bright and curious baby, and this continued. Both Shankar and I will never forget when she was around one year old and we visited our friends.

'Goodbye,' they waved to her just as we were leaving.

'Goodbye. You must come to our house as well,' she said confidently. A full sentence at that age was unusual for a baby, but she had a natural love of people even then. If she saw schoolchildren walk by the house, her face would be pressed up against the window with her small fingers pointing. 'Please can you take me to school with them?' she asked.

When Sneh, our third and final child arrived, the drama happened before he entered the world. Patna was renowned for its flooding during monsoons, and as we lived on the first floor, I became concerned that if I went into labour, wading out and getting to the hospital would be impossible.

'How am I going to manage?' I worriedly asked Shankar. I was almost full-term, and I watched anxiously from the veranda as the level of muddy brown water rose in the streets, and people drifted past on boats and floats.

To prepare, Shankar brought towels and sterile equipment home from his work. Having spent a week in obstetrics as a trainee, he reckoned that if the worst came to the worst, he could deliver the baby himself. Nearby, there was a couple who were gynaecologists, and they also offered to make their way through the water to assist.

Fortunately, the flood had subsided by the time I eventually went into labour. Now, we still laugh about how we arrived at the hospital. Shankar drove me through the streets of Patna on the back of his scooter, bumping over the potholes and weaving his way in between the cars, rickshaws and tuk-tuks. Even his professor at the hospital was angry with him.

'How did you arrive?' she asked, surprised.

'On the scooter!' Shankar confessed. In those days, it was the only way. Some days, if we went for ice cream as a family, all five of us would balance on the scooter: Shankar up front, driving, while I perched on the back holding Sneh on my lap. Sheel would also be at the front clutching the handlebars, with Shalini sandwiched in the middle.

With three children under five years old at home, I threw myself into motherhood. I was house-proud even if I could not afford the luxuries of my childhood, and I enjoyed spending time with my children. I taught them from an early age. But Shankar's plan had always been to travel, and when Shalini was around five, he applied to go to the UK to continue his work and his studies with a plan to come back to India when they were complete.

At first, neither I nor the children were allowed to travel with Shankar. Instead, he needed to travel first to the UK and begin an attachment for his medical training in Birmingham. Then, when he could prove he had the funds to support us, we could fly.

Only a few months after Shankar had made the same journey, I travelled to Kolkata to pick up my visa carrying Shankar's letter from his supervisor in Birmingham confirming his salary. At 25 years old, that train journey was the only time I had ever left Bihar. With its grand colonial buildings, Kolkata was everything I had seen in Bollywood films. I also saw escalators for the first time in my life, and I could not believe that you just had to step on the moving staircase, and it automatically took you up or down.

We flew from Delhi some weeks later – just myself with Shalini, Sheel and Sneh, who were naturally excited about travelling. If I felt sad about leaving India, I do not remember. In my mind, I would be back in a year or so to see my family and feel India's dusty soil beneath my feet once again. England was calling but not for long. As the plane touched down at Heathrow, I had no idea how England would reshape me.

Our wedding ceremony on 19th of February 1967

Just after our marriage leaving my parental home with the traditional veil on, behind my groom

Entering my new home to begin our lifelong journey together

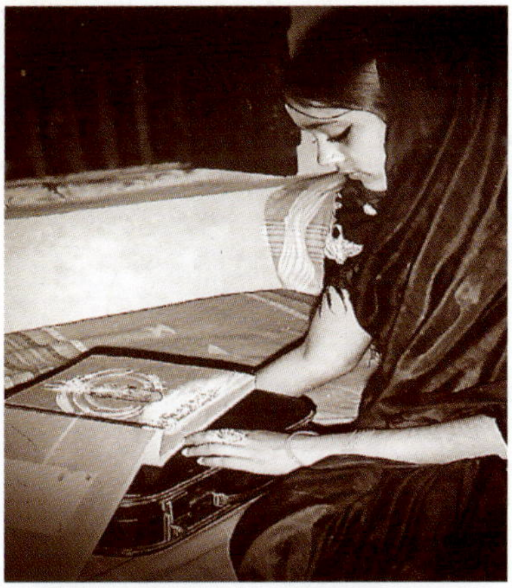

Admiring our wedding album presented to us by a very close friend whom we fondly called Sanwar bhaiya

Admiring the beauty and style of Sadhana a superstar of Hindi cinema during the 1960s

Four years after our marriage a few romantic moments of our honeymoon at Hundru Falls in Ranchi

My most favourite coat, Shankar bought me for the first time from Patna market

One of our most favourite photographs taken on our fifth wedding anniversary

My respected father- and mother-in-laws, late Sri Janaki Prasad Khemka and Srimati Rama Devi, with their baby granddaughter Shalini at our home in Patna in 1973

3
Life's Adventure

'You have to dream before your dreams can come true'

Dr. APJ Kalam

Occasionally, I think about what my life would have been like had I stayed in India. I picture myself as a very well-dressed housewife. Shankar would no doubt be a surgeon. We would live a comfortable life by Indian standards. I would spend my time shopping and looking glamorous but ultimately, I would be confined to home. I would have accepted this as my destiny, as other Indian women do.

The idea that I could ever rise through the ranks of a career to become a Dame would have been an alien concept to me – as alien as it was when I touched down at terminal three in Heathrow in late January 1978.

Thankfully, Shankar was in the arrival hall waiting for me. The flight from Delhi had been long, and the children had been sick and restless. Nevertheless, the passengers had been understanding, and I got through it. When we walked through customs, I carried one suitcase between us, and I spoke no English. The children were so excited to see their papa. They ran towards him and hugged him tightly as I took in my new surroundings with curiosity. My temporary home was bright and advanced – a world away from the Bihar I had left behind.

Shankar was now based in Birmingham at the Royal Orthopaedic Hospital, south of the city centre. After his initial assessment in Doncaster, where he had impressed senior colleagues, he had been allowed to apply for jobs. He was offered two: one in Darlington, which would have commanded a higher salary, and the other in Birmingham, which as a teaching hospital, held more prestige. He opted for Birmingham.

On the afternoon of our arrival, we boarded a coach at Victoria Station. The cold winter wind whipped around us, and there was snow covering the ground. I had never seen snow before, and from the coach window, I looked out with amazement at how it blanketed the vast English countryside.

Shankar had rented a three-bedroom house on Hole Farm Road in the pleasant suburb of Northfield, not far from the hospital. It was a neat property with a large living room and a back garden – so different to our apartment in Patna. Upstairs, the bathroom had a bathtub – the first I had ever seen. In India, we used a bucket and water jug to wash. A television was unheard of back home. In my family home in Riga or at my grandmother's house, only the radio played the BBC World Service, even though as a young girl, I did not understand what was being said.

At first, I could not get used to the quietness of the street. In Patna, all we could hear was the beeping of horns and the revving of engines. In our apartment, family members and household helpers came and went – the door was always open. On Hole Farm Road, the streets were empty. People kept themselves to themselves, and no household had any help. Washing and cleaning was done by families themselves – mainly women. Even gardening and DIY were considered a hobby.

For example, I had naturally assumed that as Shankar had rented the property from the hospital, it would take care of the lawn, but that did not happen. Instead, we were given a mechanical lawnmower, which I did try to operate on a couple of occasions but without much success. In the end, neighbours complained because the seeds from the long grass kept blowing into their gardens and populating the soil. After that, we admitted defeat and asked the hospital to send someone.

That said, our neighbours were very welcoming. Being in a white, middle-class suburb, we lived separately to other Asian or minority communities in Birmingham, who would have inhabited areas such as Smethwick or Handsworth and whose families would have entered Britain in the post-1947 migration from India and Pakistan. Even in Shankar's work, he was the lone Asian man. All the other staff were white.

If there was any racism, I did not notice. Generally, I found people very friendly. However, at that time, I was unaware of the nuances of British society or the class system. In fact, when I arrived and made my way through London on that first day, everyone looked the same to me. In my bewilderment, I could not differentiate between rich or poor, working class or middle class or any other person, which I am sure worked in my favour.

For the children, the experience was perhaps a little different. Shalini and Sheel settled in better than Sneh, who missed India so much. In particular, he missed our home help in Patna called Sunaina, who had often taken care of the children, and Sneh asked and cried for her on many occasions.

Next door in Northfield lived an elderly couple called Mr and Mrs Harvey, who knocked on our door to welcome us in that first week. Then, two doors down, there was the family of one of Shankar's colleagues, who also became good friends. His wife, Jenny, came to my house to introduce herself, and she even started to teach me a little English.

'Asha, speak English to your children at home. And also, when you are outside, try to speak English,' she advised me. At first, I found it hard, but I forced myself. When the television was on, I regularly sat in front of the children's programme *Playschool* with the kids and learned alongside them.

Soon, Shalini was enrolled in primary school and Sheel at nursery. Sneh was still too young, but I took him to local playgroups, where I mixed with other young mums. Every morning, I battled through the winter weather dressed in my sari and chappal shoes, slipping and sliding on the ice and feeling the bitter chill of a British February. My bones ached!

As I remember, I had one coat bought for me by Shankar in Patna Market, but that was all. Although as a married woman I would have worn nothing but a sari back home, in England, it became impractical given the freezing cold. Gradually, when we had the money, we ventured into Birmingham city centre – to the Bull Ring Market and the department stores – to buy trousers, jumpers and jackets to keep us warm.

I will never forget struggling on the bus with three children armed with milk chocolate digestive biscuits to give them energy as we shopped. There were times when I was so tired that I came home sick with exhaustion. In those days, we did not have a car. To stock up on Indian food and maybe also to remind ourselves of home, we travelled to the district of Handsworth on the bus. Along Soho Road, we could find chapati flour and basmati rice, Indian spices and lentils that were impossible to find in any English supermarket.

How we managed, I am not sure. Shankar had arrived in England with £3 – the maximum amount he was allowed to bring in currency. I had been allowed the same. His trainee salary was not high – around £180 per month – and so we budgeted to make ends meet. Instead of spending it on ourselves, we ploughed everything into our children and prioritised our spending around giving them the best start in life.

As they began school, I made sure their uniforms were immaculate. Their shoes were polished within an inch of their life. Every evening, I would lay out their pristine clothing ready for their morning lessons, and I always recall how teachers would comment on how well-turned-out they were. Just as I had done in Sitamarhi, my kids stood out as something special.

Although I made friends with many of the teachers, I also managed to upset a few. Several teachers did not like that I taught the children at home as a way of pushing them further and complementing their lessons. All three children could recite their 20 times table and everything in between by the time they got to primary school. In the teachers' minds, children running ahead of the class was not a positive, but I ignored this. At home, no one had been able to tell me what to do, and this did not change when I got to England. Besides, I did not agree. Both Shankar and I were competitive people. We have a drive that we recognise in each other, and we wanted our children to be the brightest. Now, with hindsight and having mellowed a little, perhaps I would not have been so ambitious for Shalini, Sheel and Sneh. We were young, and naturally, we wanted the best.

With time, Shankar and I were able to afford a little more, but even then, our funds were limited. On one occasion, we wanted to spoil the children and take them to an Indian restaurant. The Gaylord was situated on New Street, not far from Birmingham's museum and art galleries. Owned by the BBC presenter Mahendra Kaul, the chain had sprung up in the 1970s, and Shankar had eaten there with his work colleagues on a department night out. It felt like such a special treat. As we arrived, we were seated in the waiting area while a table became free. Bombay mix was brought for us, and we were asked to look at the menu.

'Look at the price!' I said to Shankar. For a buffet meal, it was around £10 a head, way above what we could afford.

'We can't eat here,' I said, and Shankar agreed. That amount was almost a quarter of his monthly salary. Embarrassedly, we left the restaurant and headed home.

'Why can't we go?' the children kept crying, but they were far too young to understand that for us, that money was way beyond our means.

Now, when I think about it, every day was a school day for those first few months in England. Simple things like watching spring turn to summer and the nights get lighter filled us with amazement, and we were learning and growing together. 'How can the sun still be shining at 10 p.m.?' we asked. In India, the sun sets on the horizon by 6 p.m., even in the summer months. Also, there was no particular etiquette around elders. Back home, it was respectful to cover our heads and call elders aunt or uncle – never by their first names. And kissing in the street! For me, this was a proper culture shock – a phenomenon that would not have been allowed in India. In all honesty, it is something that I have never got used to. For us, kissing was a private show of affection, not something to be seen in public.

Otherwise, I was beginning to notice the freedoms people had in the UK. Although not every woman I knew worked, some had jobs. Others, who I met at coffee mornings or around the children's swimming clubs and tennis clubs, could drive. They were not confined to a kitchen or necessarily ground down by a domestic life. Every day, I learned a little more about English culture, about the opportunities open to people, about English politics, about its geography, and I saw how I could flourish and blossom in a way I would not have been able to in Bihar.

Even so, the late seventies were a turbulent time in British history. Just as we moved from Birmingham, Margaret Thatcher was elected as prime minister. In the run-up to the election – the first year we had arrived in the UK – there had been the Winter of Discontent, characterised by widespread industrial strikes across Britain. Recession ate at the country's fabric, but for us – even at a time of financial crisis – the standard of living in the UK was far better than what we had left behind.

As we were adjusting to our new surroundings, I often thought of home, yet I had little desire to return. Looking back, I realised that I had found marrying so young and having to integrate into Shankar's more traditional family rather traumatic. Of course, Shankar's family had treated me with nothing but love and affection, but any expectation that I would find myself or develop myself in life was low.

That said, I did miss my grandmother, and I thought about her often. And I missed our circle of friends in Patna. I regularly sent back pictures of our new life and the children. By then, my father had had three more children with his second wife and was busy looking after them. My brothers were also pursuing their own careers, and my brother Suresh, with whom I remained very close, had met and fallen in love with a Keralan girl he had met in Ranchi. As telephone calls were so expensive at that time, writing letters became the only way we could communicate.

Months in England went by, and before we knew it, these turned into years. In order to progress his career, Shankar needed to move around hospitals, each time taking a more senior post. In Birmingham, he had impressed the consultant, Mr Harrison, so much that he and his wife often came to dinner at our house, and we would be invited to go out with them for a vegetarian meal.

'We would never dream of being invited to socialise with Max Harrison!' Shankar's senior colleagues told him, such was the hierarchy of the medical profession. But Shankar had a natural ability to charm people. He was hard-working and always eager to learn and progress. He moved effortlessly from one job to another.

His first posting outside of Birmingham was in Stourbridge, a pretty English market town, west of the city. There, he became a registrar, and we moved with him again into rented hospital accommodation. This meant the children had to move school again, which became a frequent occurrence over the next few years. However, they seemed to adapt well to their changing circumstances and integrate into each new class.

In Stourbridge, I began to step out further into the wide world. My English improved, and as time progressed, I began to develop myself in other ways. I started to learn how to drive in Stourbridge. It had taken Shankar five attempts to pass his test, but eventually, he bought a sea-green Renault 18, and I saw further freedom to take advantage of.

We also made new friends there. Mrs Rees, who was Shalini's teacher at the local school, became a family friend, and she and her husband often came to socialise. Perhaps unconsciously, I was always keen to befriend the teachers so that the children would have a guardian looking after them, but I also believe it was my way of integrating into a foreign country. I wanted their lives to be as smooth as possible while we remained in the UK. At that time, we still planned to go home when Shankar was fully trained.

When we moved to Wallasey on Merseyside in 1980, I taught myself to swim. I regularly took the children to after-school swimming clubs and watched from the balcony as they were instructed on breaststroke and front crawl. As they splashed around in the water below, I made note of everything the teacher was telling them. When it came to me getting in the water for the first time, it was under my own steam rather than as part of a class. I almost drowned! The next time, I kept my head above water, and slowly, I improved.

At Wallasey, however, I had my first real experience of racism. Up until then, I felt people noticing our difference, but usually this was done affectionately. For example, when Sneh started school, there were always comments about how light-skinned he was – how could he possibly be our son when we were very clearly Asian? But as I say, this was friendly.

This particular incident happened at the children's swimming club. One woman, who was English but had been visiting from Australia, had said something to me under her breath while she looked me up and down. Then, she very blatantly refused to sit beside me.

'How could someone be so hurtful?' I thought. It wounded me, even though I knew that racism was her problem and her issue rather than anything I had done.

Eventually, when we moved again to Southport, a pretty coastal town north of Liverpool, I passed my driving test after only two attempts. There, we often enjoyed running on the beach. In fact, we settled in so much that it was here that our affection for England really started to grow. By now, Shankar had the desire and capability to move up the ranks to become a consultant, even though many of his Asian contemporaries had left and gone into general practice. To specialise, he needed to complete his master's qualification, which he did at Liverpool University. However, we continued to move.

It was in Fleetwood, a well-heeled area north of Blackpool, that I really started to find my feet. With the children settled in another school, I had a little time during the day to think further about how I might develop myself.

Near Fleetwood Hospital, there was an administrative office, and every time I passed by it, a thought crossed my mind. Perhaps I could go in and ask for a job? One day, I very nearly turned to enter the office, but I froze on the spot and stared at the building's double doors. For some reason, I stopped myself. 'What job would I ask for?' I thought. Other than my schooling back in Bihar, I had no academic skills. By now, I had a decent grasp of spoken English, but my written English was not there at all. Besides, I had never thought of a career or what I might do given the chance of one.

'Asha. You can ask for a job, but you'll need some skills first,' I told myself. At first, I enrolled on a typing course at the Blackpool and Fylde College of Further and Higher Education, thinking that perhaps in the future, I may be able to help Shankar with his practice administration. Certainly, from the moment I started my studies, I had tunnel vision. All that concerned me was my family, their achievements, their success, my journey and my learning. Everything else paled into insignificance.

We bought a second-hand typewriter, and every day, I would get up early and touch-type. While the children were at school, I continued practising. I learned everything I needed to know in record time. In my mind, I was the best. 'I have to be the best. I have to be first,' I kept telling myself. Perhaps, given my supportive upbringing in India, I never felt that I was not good enough. It was not the need to get better that propelled me forward. Instead, my inner voice was always telling me, 'I must get distinctions to prove to myself and others that I am an achiever'.

If I was the focus of some resentment in the class, I ignored it. If people wanted to be my friend, then I welcomed that. In all honesty, I was so focussed that it did not matter to me what other people thought. What I did think about often was how if I had been back home, I would never have had any opportunity to do any course, even if it was a typing course. Not only were there no vocational courses for mature students like myself, but women would have had no chance to take them. Fortunately, I was very lucky to be supported by Shankar and my children in whatever I did.

Fleetwood was to be a growing experience for all of us, but we returned to Birmingham for a short six-month spell. There, the children excelled at school so much that the headteacher, Mr Newey, came to our house one evening to talk to us about Sheel. There was some concern that he was so ahead of his classmates that he was difficult to teach, and there had been some comments about this from his class teacher.

'He is very bright. Have you considered sending him to a private school?' Mr Newey suggested.

'I would be happy to send him to a private school, but I do not have that kind of money,' Shankar replied.

Mr Newey had been a teacher at Caldicott Prep School in Buckinghamshire before teaching in Birmingham. He thought Sheel would easily pass the assessment to get in, but he also told us that if funds were short, he could apply for a scholarship and have three quarters of the fee paid for him. That would still be an expensive affair for us, what with school uniform, hat, sports kit and so on, but it was one that we could manage if we budgeted.

Sheel was around nine years old when we took him to be assessed. After an exam, which he passed easily, he was offered a place, and he became the first of our children who we waved off to boarding school. While he seemed to cope very well with the separation, I found those early weeks and months hard. When we dropped him off, I felt excitement at his achievement, mixed with a churning sickness in my stomach. I was always worrying about him, even though I still had my hands full with Shalini and Sneh, and I looked forward to when we could be reunited as a family again.

Fortunately, Sheel came back for half-term and the holidays, which we always enjoyed together. In fact, when we were in Fleetwood, we decided that if we were to return to India, we would like to see Europe first. However, any trip to the continent would be complicated. We are vegetarian, and in the early eighties, it was difficult enough to find vegetarian food on any menu in the UK. This was going to be doubly hard abroad. Then, Shankar had an idea.

'Why don't we take a caravan on a European tour?' he suggested. I was keen, even though he had never driven on the right-hand side of the road before, and he had only ever driven a caravan once to the Lake District. Mr Torrence, one of the consultants at Shankar's work, owned a caravan, so Shankar asked him for some advice.

'I'm thinking about taking a caravan across the Channel,' he told him.

'Why don't you just go to the top of Blackpool Tower and throw yourself off?' he laughed. He said Shankar must be mad to even consider such a holiday, but Shankar was stubborn.

'If I am mad, then you are a coward. And if you have never taken your caravan across the Channel, then you should give it to me to drive there,' he said jokingly. Then, he went out and hired a five-berth caravan and started planning our route.

For six weeks that summer, we toured through France, Switzerland, Italy, Luxembourg and Germany. Manoeuvring a five-berth caravan through the busy streets of Paris with traffic whizzing around us was an experience in itself. In Rome, sharing the roads with Italian drivers was almost as chaotic as being back home in India! All along the journey, we home-cooked in our makeshift kitchen: matar kulcha, bhajis and samosas, to name a few dishes. In Interlaken in Switzerland, which is nestled between the soaring Bernese Alps and surrounded by crystal-clear waters, we picked corn from a cornfield and served corn on the cob.

We felt very proud that despite Mr Torrence's predictions, we had not had any serious incidents on the road – but we spoke too soon. Our one disaster came in Switzerland when Shankar attempted a steep mountain pass. The car groaned in first gear for what felt like miles. We felt the weight of the five-berth caravan pulling us back, and the engine struggled the steeper we climbed. In the rear-view mirror, we could see a queue of traffic snaking behind us, with some drivers becoming so impatient they beeped their horns and tried to overtake us, somewhat perilously.

Then, as its engine coughed and spluttered, the car stopped dead.

'What are we going to do?' we asked each other. The children were restless, and by now, we were all a little panicked.

'If we call the RAC or the AA, it will take them two days to come!' Shankar said. In an attempt to cool the engine down, he opened up the bonnet and let it breathe for an hour or so while furious drivers shouted from their windows. In a last-ditch attempt, he prayed to God that the car would start. By some miracle, when he turned the ignition, it did, and we were finally able to reach the top – the deities had been on our side that day!

As the children grew further, so did my sense of independence. I had delighted in looking after them, but with Sheel away at boarding school and my typing course under my belt, I looked to what else I could do to enhance my development.

When we moved to the Welsh seaside town of Rhyl, Shankar took a job at the teaching hospital at St Asaph. Meanwhile, I decided to enrol myself in an information technology teaching course. The course was for mature students, and examinations were overseen by the WJEC, one of Wales's main examining bodies. The body caters for mainstream academic subjects but also specialises in vocational training, such as apprenticeships, professional courses and part-time study.

The course at the community-based Llandudno College in Colwyn Bay, now called Coleg Llandrillo, would open up an opportunity for me to teach technology to adults in a further education context. It covered the principles of teaching alongside the basics of technology and computer science.

I still remember the large and cumbersome BBC computers in the teaching rooms and the CD-ROM drives that were needed to save any word-processing documents. Nowadays, of course, this is all second nature to so many people, and technology has moved on apace, but this was around 1985. Technology was clunky and alien to beginners, and email had not yet been invented. My job was to help students navigate a way through.

In many ways, taking that adult education course was not only the beginning of me blossoming as a person, but it also started quietly shaping my ideas around education. It struck me that not everybody was cut out to follow an academic path. Also, it instilled in me the notion that you are never too old to learn. I was in my early thirties when I started the two-year part-time study, and I would continue on the path of learning for many years.

The course allowed me to study but also to be at home when Shalini and Sneh arrived home from school. Juggling motherhood and study became part of my daily routine. What struck me most was that in Britain, I could be from anywhere and at any age with children and still be able to progress in life provided that I took the opportunities available to me.

I also took to teaching very naturally. I developed patience with those who I was teaching, but I also enjoyed the performance of standing in front of a class. I loved the feeling of power to shape outcomes and other people's progress. Again, I had the same determination to prove I was the best as when I took my typing course. Out of the eight or so fellow students on the course, I became the only person to pass it – an achievement I am still very proud of.

The longer Shankar and I remained in the UK, the more established I became in my studies. Also, the more settled the children became at school, the more our plans to move back to India receded into the background. We had not been home for eight years, and it would be another two years before we set foot on Bihar's sprawling plains again. Just as we were contemplating putting down roots in our adopted home, India was still reeling from the aftermath of a turbulent period that had culminated in the assassination of Prime Minister Indira Gandhi in 1984. As a country, India had not yet found its way to becoming a powerhouse. Yet, we were finding our way thousands of miles from home.

Young Shalini, Sheel and Sneh dressed in the traditional Rajasthani costume. These photographs were taken during a family wedding just before we left India

Meeting Mr Max Harrison, a senior consultant orthopaedic surgeon at the Royal orthopaedic hospital in Birmingham during the summer fete soon after our arrival in the UK. Mr Harrison became very fond of our children and we regarded him as our guardian

The cutest trio Shalini, Sheel and Sneh in their school photograph at Southport

Kids having fun and enjoying the rugged beauty of the Lake District during our holiday

Shalini, Sheel and Sneh showing off their swimming medals and trophies in Southport with their proud coach in 1981

At Lands End we were amused to find how far is Patna from there

Shalini, Sheel and Sneh looking proud to be photographed with the cricket legend, Sir Ian Botham, in 1984

What an adventure! Me towing a five-berth caravan on the Swiss mountains

4

Dawn of a New Era

'Desire is the key to motivation, but it's determination and commitment to an unrelenting pursuit of your goal - a commitment to excellence - that will enable you to attain the success you seek'

Mario Andretti

In 1986, Shankar and I realised the inevitable and put down roots in England. We had been in the UK for eight years. He was progressing well in his career, our children were settled at school, and I had also made the first steps on my journey of self-discovery.

So, when Shankar got a job as a trainee registrar on rotation with a world-renowned orthopaedic hospital in Oswestry, we bought a house in the environs of that quaint Shropshire town. A historic and picturesque location on the Welsh border, it was to be our base for the next 13 years. By this time, our youngest son, Sneh, had also passed his scholarship exam and was boarding at Heath Mount School in Stevenage. Likewise, Shalini got a scholarship to Moreton Hall, a reputable private school that was closer to home, and she started as a day boarder.

Our new home was a modest three-bedroomed detached house in a suburban cul-de-sac. It was not a palace, but we made it our own. As neither of us was good at DIY, our neighbours Di and Gerry, who were both nurses, helped us to put up wallpaper that we bought from Laura Ashley. Shankar decorated with surgical precision, and I hung beautiful curtains. Shankar even indulged his love of snooker when we bought a three-quarter length table, which we placed in our games room. A snooker table was always a feature of the films that we loved, and Shankar had one seared in his memory from a childhood visit to the home of a celebrated industrialist in Bihar. It became his very first status symbol.

With our home complete and the children settled, I looked to see what I could do next. I had my typing course and a teaching qualification under my belt. Now, I wanted a job. Oswestry College was a ten-minute walk from our house, and one day – as I was passing – I walked in. Inside, I approached the receptionist. I had not planned what I was going to say, but suddenly, I found myself enquiring about a job.

'Could I see the principal, please?' I asked.

'What for?' the receptionist looked up.

'I'd like a job,' I said matter-of-factly.

I could see she was taken aback, and she politely explained that jobs were advertised. If I wanted to apply for one, the college would happily consider me for a role. But I did not take no for an answer.

'I really would like to talk to the principal,' I pressed her.

It must have been fate because as I was standing there, the college principal stepped forward from his office. He had been listening in on the conversation.

'Hello. I'm Shaun McLaughlin,' he said, holding out his hand. 'Who are you?'

'I'm Asha Khemka, and I'm here to ask about a job.'

'Please, come and have a seat in my office,' he ushered me through. I could not believe my luck.

I explained to Mr McLaughlin everything that I had done and that I was keen to start work.

'I can see you are ambitious and want to achieve – where do you see yourself in a few years' time?' he asked. The question took me by surprise, so I had to think on my feet.

'I hadn't thought about it until now, but seeing you in that seat, that's where I want to be,' I said boldly.

'You have a job. You start on Monday,' he smiled at me.

My job covered the administrative duties in the office of the college. It was at the bottom rung of the career ladder, but it was my first job, and I was proud of it. Admittedly, I did not like a lot of the work and found it below my capability. Occasionally, if I complained, I would be met with comments like, 'If this is your job, you have to do it,' from my superior. What made it harder was the knowledge that my husband was excelling at his job, and my children were in the top boarding schools in the country, but I carried on knowing that the only person who could elevate myself was me.

With time, the work started to grind on me, as did taking orders. I needed to challenge myself further. As my job was part-time, I looked at how I might obtain a degree. It had always been in the back of my mind that I would like to go to university and that I had the ability to do so. My experience so far was in teaching, and so I sought out a Bachelor of Education course but with a focus on teaching business studies. When I told Shaun McLaughlin and his deputy Ron Pugh what my plans were, they immediately gave me their support – support that continued throughout my whole career at Oswestry College.

The part-time degree course was at the North Wales Institute of Further and Higher Education in Wrexham and was awarded through Cardiff University, its affiliated university. In order to get a place, I needed to complete an access course, but I managed this with relative ease and a lot of support from my children! As Shankar was working much of the time, Ron even drove me to lectures and tutorials on days when I had no transport. Juggling work at Oswestry, my course in Wrexham and running a home became a constant balancing act.

Meanwhile, in the summer of 1988, Shankar and I decided to return to India with the children, albeit on holiday. It had been a full ten years since we had left our homeland, and although we were always in contact through letters, it seemed the right time to recalibrate and see our families again.

Naturally, the children were very excited to be back in the place of their birth. However, the journey was tempered by my getting sick not long after we touched down in Delhi. This was a novel feeling for me. I likened myself to a British tourist acclimatising to Indian food and water for the first time, struck down by the infamous Delhi belly.

Immediately, I noted how different our lives had become when compared to Delhi's teeming streets, the market stalls and the thousands of people on the roadsides. This feeling only intensified as we made our way to Bihar. While everything seemed so familiar in India, I also had a feeling of separation. I had changed. I had a newfound inner confidence that many people commented on. 'You are glowing, Asha,' they told me. They were right. I looked different to the 25-year-old woman I had been when I left. Back then, I had been so busy with a young family in Patna that I had no time to spend on myself, but now, the glamour of my youth was starting to return.

I was also different intellectually. Whereas the women in our families were still confined to the home, I had grown, developed and flourished. Because of this, I found some of the conversations around the minutiae of domestic life hard to join in with, and the gulf between my old life and my new world seemed to deepen. What also struck me was how physically hard some of my relatives' lives were compared to mine. Whereas before I would have sat on the floor rolling chapati dough easily, this was now back-breaking work for me. I struggled, and the sweat dripped from my forehead in the monsoon heat. I also struggled with the way that women were put down by their society – by men especially – and how the caste system resigned people to their fate. How lucky I was that in Britain and with the support of my family, I was able to shine.

Of course, the children loved being there, and they were spoiled by both our families during the whole stay. They did not want to leave. In a strange way, they felt they belonged, even though most of their lives had been spent in England. Now they were old enough, we also wanted to show them the sheer majesty of India. So, as well as spending time in Sitamarhi and Patna, we travelled with family to the hot springs in Rajgir, a holy pilgrimage site. We also visited the Himalayan foothills, to Darjeeling, and wound our way through tea plantations nestled in the shadow of Mount Kanchenjunga.

Watching the sunrise dance across Kanchenjunga from the vantage point of the Tiger Hills is a moment of beauty that still lingers in our memories. The changing hues of violet, red, pink and orange combined with the early morning sunlight sparkling off the snow-capped mountain peak and its gleaming latticework of glaciers was mesmerising. As the sun transformed from a small yolk to a burning orange ball in the sky and the cold night air subsided, we felt its warmth on our skins. Nature had enchanted us and reminded us what it is to be human, as has every journey to India since.

At around the same time, Shankar and I were forced to rescind our Indian passports when we took British citizenship. Relations between India and the UK were strained at the time, and so, sadly, dual citizenship was not an option. We had heavy hearts in doing so. Although the direction of our lives had changed, we remained Indian to our core. More recently, I have been fortunate enough to build professional ties with our homeland as well as travelling there frequently with Shankar, but this was not the case then.

Back in the UK, I returned to my studies. Sheel had also won an academic scholarship to Harrow, where he was to start that autumn. Naturally, Shankar and I were incredibly proud. Harrow was one of the top private schools in the country, and Sheel had got there on his own merit. We would still have to pay 25% of his fees, but with Shankar progressing through the ranks and me continuing to work at Oswestry College, this was affordable.

A couple of years later, Sneh would follow Sheel to Harrow, also on a scholarship. With hindsight, Sneh struggled far more with being away from home, but we were young and ambitious for our children and proud of their achievements. Given our time again, I would probably think twice before sending my children to boarding school.

Not long after I started my degree course, I moved from my secretarial job in the college to a teaching role. Not only was I teaching further education students, but I was also sent out on placements with local secondary schools to teach a business studies course. Funnily enough, these children made me anxious. Their grasp of English was far better than mine, and many of them were more knowledgeable than me. To give myself authority and respect in the classroom, I prepared and over-prepared – a routine that came to serve me well over the next few years.

Although these were the first schoolchildren I had taught, I treated them much like I did my own children. Discipline was at the heart of my classroom. They had to listen, and if they misbehaved, they were treated to a hard stare. However, I went out of my way to understand them, and I had an affectionate relationship with them, as I remember.

In Oswestry, I moved from my role in administration to that of a part-time lecturer. As well as teaching the students their chosen subject, I also taught them how to present themselves with authority, as I believe this is also important in life. Besides, if I had not walked into the college and asked for a job, I would never have got one.

'Opportunity is waiting for you if you have the drive and the hunger. If I can do it, you can do it too,' I told them.

However, I did not have quite the same inner confidence when I got a phone call from the principal one day. There was a job on offer as the college coordinator of business studies, and he wanted to offer it to me.

'Why? And how?' I asked. I was not experienced in many of the things the role required.

'We believe you can do it if you put your mind to it,' Mr McLaughlin said.

My brief was to sort out some of the problems in the department with a goal to raise overall standards. This required me to develop a broad overview of teaching methods and the resources available and to identify where changes could be made. Admittedly, it was a tough time. Not everybody in the college liked my appointment, especially not people who had been my superiors in my previous roles there. However, I ignored this. I had the support of the senior management team, and that was all that mattered to me.

Nevertheless, I found the job challenging. It was my first step up to looking at the college from a strategic vantage point. To prove myself, I worked doubly hard to evidence all the changes I recommended the college should make. That way, I knew my work could not be dismissed. Perhaps as an outsider and a woman, I was extra diligent. I also found I could use my multitasking skills to my advantage. Thankfully, my efforts did not go unnoticed. Even the head of the college teachers' union, who had initially been resistant to my taking on the role, came to respect me. Before I met him, I knew very little about what unions did. I had never been a member of one, and it took me a while to appreciate the role they can play in protecting workers.

Mostly, common sense guided me. I had run a household for 20 years – its own kind of institution. I knew that if I gave staff ownership of their duties, coupled with trust and support, then this would lead to them feeling more fulfilled at work. Of course, giving staff ownership had to be balanced by accountability and targets to meet.

Meanwhile, I graduated with a 2:1 in my business studies teaching degree – a proud moment for me and the Khemka family. Attending the convocation ceremony of Cardiff University at Carnarvon Castle with my family and friends was a special occasion – something I had always wanted to experience. I felt a sense of accomplishment, a feeling that elevated my self-esteem and boosted my enthusiasm to keep moving forwards on the path I had chosen.

During the same period, Shankar was having to travel for his work. After his job in Rhyl, he worked in Oswestry itself before embarking on two years in Wrexham. In the year following our trip to India, he took up a post in Manchester and began a constant rotation of early commutes. The upside of this meant I had time to continue with my studies and work. In many ways, I had the best of both worlds. Even though Shankar's constant travel and high-pressure job took up much of his energy, it was necessary if he were ever to reach the post of consultant, which had been our dream.

In Manchester, he was lucky. Not long after he arrived, the post of locum consultant became available following a resignation. Shankar was asked to take up the job. Manchester was then followed by a stint in Ayrshire in Scotland and later six months in Bath, as well as a further three years as a locum consultant in Dudley, West Midlands.

At Oswestry College, my role as co-ordinator had gone well. With dedication and perseverance, I had turned the department's woes around. This gave me added confidence to apply for the job of head of department in business studies when it came up – a role that I now considered myself as having a good chance of being appointed to. The shortlist was between two people: myself and one other woman.

My interview went well, but when the job was handed to my colleague, I found it very hard to accept. I went to see the principal.

'Why did she get the job?' I asked him. My disappointment was palpable. While I knew I had the support of Shaun McLaughlin, and although I did not take the knock-back personally, I believed in my heart that I had been the best candidate.

'We felt she would bond better with people,' he replied. Maybe my forthrightness was not everybody's cup of tea and popularity mattered, but that wounded me. I did not want to be better liked to excel at work. I wanted to be good and to make a difference. In all honesty, I was not in a place to accept that decision for some time, but I picked myself up and carried on, and perhaps this gave me an added drive to prove my worth.

At this point in my career, I also began to take an interest in the broader aspect of education beyond the confinement of the classroom and college boundaries. I needed to broaden my horizons to see how I could further add to my skillset. A deep inner desire to be in a position to make a difference – to the wider world of education – led me to train to be an Ofsted inspector. Ofsted, the Government's Office for Standards in Education, is tasked with inspecting schools and colleges and advising them on how to elevate standards. I became interested in how it inspected colleges, what criteria it made its assessments on and the ways in which the college could prepare for its inspection. Not only did I learn so much, but my Ofsted training gave me a further string to my bow. Following my training, I was regularly called to inspect business studies departments in a variety of colleges.

Whenever I returned to my college after inspecting another college, I put myself in the inspector's shoes and challenged the college based on the same evidence that would be laid out in front of Ofsted. I began seeing the college with fresh eyes and knew that if there was a single loophole in my rationale, I could be challenged.

I also applied to be on the board of the Business Studies Institute, an organisation that looked at all aspects of the curriculum. It also provided a good networking opportunity for me in my field of expertise. Again, I was very fortunate to have Shankar's support. If I needed to go to a meeting or attend a conference, he never stopped me. On one occasion when I was required to attend a meeting in Durham, Shankar drove me there and back, battling through driving snow and fog, just so I could be there. Shankar accompanied me on so many journeys, just so I did not miss out. I am forever grateful for his encouragement; he has been a pillar of support throughout.

Intimate dinner with Heather and Shaun McLaughlin, Principal of Oswestry College at their home in Shropshire

My first teaching session with an adult student in a community college in Shropshire

A photograph taken at my graduation ceremony of Cardiff University at Carnarvon Castle in 1992

With Shalini at Moreton Hall at her award ceremony here

With two Harrovians Sheel and Sneh at their speech day at Harrow School

Celebrating our silver wedding anniversary with friends and family in Glasgow in 1992

5
Learning to Lead

'Leadership and learning are indispensable to each other'

John F Kennedy

In 1994, Shankar got the call we had been waiting for all of his career. We were in Norway together, as I was attending a conference there. On the other end of the line was the senior consultant at Queen's Hospital in the Staffordshire town of Burton-on-Trent asking him to come for an interview. Shankar had applied for the job there, but this had followed several disappointments elsewhere. Back then, the higher echelons of the medical profession were mainly populated by white, male consultants. Although Shankar had excelled in all his positions, the final step up to be a substantive consultant had so far been met with rejection.

Admittedly, there were times when we almost accepted defeat. So many of Shankar's Asian contemporaries had come up against the same barriers and taken staff-grade jobs. The glass ceiling seemed impossible to break. One job Shankar applied for in Oxford had been particularly disappointing. After the interview, one of the representatives from the Royal College of Surgeons took him aside. 'You were the best candidate for the job,' he told Shankar. In the same breath, he admitted that the job had gone to someone else because they were local and not an outsider. Shankar found this difficult to hear.

When Shankar went for the interview at Burton-on-Trent, while his CV and performance stood out in glowing terms, by sheer chance the interviewing committee were also aware of his recent work as a locum consultant in Manchester, and he got the job. For the children and me, this was a very proud moment in the Khemka family history – one of the happiest days of our lives. It was everything Shankar and we, as a family, had been working towards.

At first, Shankar took hospital accommodation before we put the house in Oswestry up for sale. Meanwhile, I started looking for positions nearer to Burton-on-Trent. I had been at the college in Oswestry for seven years, working my way up to lecturer alongside juggling my other supplementary roles, but I was also hungry for new challenges.

Because of my networking and the extracurricular work that I had taken on, I knew of a job that had come up in Tamworth College. On paper, the role of deputy head of faculty was exactly the job I wanted. The college was sizeable, with around 700 students in the business studies faculty, and I knew the head of faculty well, as we had met at several conferences. In my mind, the job was about creating links between industry and the college; it was about overseeing the teaching and learning aspects of the college and marketing the business studies department. It was also about securing better and more fulfilling work experience for the students.

Unfortunately, the reality turned out to be very different. Not long after I started there, it became clear that this was a more administrative role. Instead of using the strategic talents I had accumulated at Oswestry, my duties were purely functional and not expansive in the way that I had hoped. For example, I was in charge of timetabling and organising sick cover. Not only did I know that this would drive me crazy, I was also at pains to understand why the college had appointed me to do it. Surely, they could have employed a good administrator at a salary lower than mine who would have done this job far more competently? My heart just was not in it.

Without going through the usual channel of my line manager, I spoke directly to the principal, Rupert Herd. He was a good man, and we were friends, so I did not think much of approaching him directly.

'Do you know what I do, Rupert?' I said as I sat in his office.

'Of course, Asha!' Rupert laughed and repeated my job title of deputy head of faculty. He seemed to have missed the point.

'Yes, Rupert. That's my title, but do you really know what I do in my job?' I asked him.

At that, Rupert reeled off a list of my duties.

'Why are you paying me this salary to do this?' I challenged him. I told him to appoint a good administrator and use me for the job I had come to do.

'You know what you are doing, Asha?' he smiled. 'You are putting yourself out of a job'.

In a sense, I was. However, I had a proposal for him. I knew that the college needed its standards driven up, and having trained as an Ofsted inspector, I knew exactly how to do this.

'I have the knowledge, and I can drive this change,' I told him. Not only could I drive that change in my own department but in every department across the college where the same staffing structure was replicated.

'The choice is yours,' I told Rupert as I left him thinking on my proposal.

Within weeks, I was made the Director of Quality – a newly created post. Perhaps unsurprisingly, this was not liked by several members of staff. Not only had I gone above managers' heads to talk to Rupert, but I had only just arrived at the college. Colleagues saw me as a threat.

How can I forget a particularly hurtful comment that came from a fellow female member of staff? 'You just have to flicker your eyelashes, and you can get people to do whatever you want,' she told me one day. I grimaced at her words. The suggestion was that I used my looks and charm to elevate myself into a more senior position rather than my skills. This made me very angry given that I had worked my way up from a typing course in Oswestry. Also upsetting for some of my colleagues was that I had asked the senior leadership team if I could join them on their regular lunches.

'Why am I not being invited? Am I not senior enough?' I joked with the Finance Director. Soon, I was joining the team. I had no fear in challenging the status quo if I felt that was the right thing to do.

When it came to my new role, I approached it in exactly the same way I had done every other job. I did my homework. I knew the college data inside out and upside down. I researched grades and retention rates. I knew how the college compared to other local colleges but also where it stood against the national average. I knew about gender parity in the college, how many students came from minority ethnic backgrounds and how the number compared to that of other student groups.

At a senior level, I understood that in order to make any changes, I needed to persuade my colleagues with an argument based on facts and figures.

I needed to understand my own business better than anyone else and put forward my case with confidence. At the same time, I was also eager to learn more, and I increased my presence on a number of boards. What I had started to do in Oswestry I continued, although it was not without disappointments. Several boards did not take up my application, but enough did. The point was that I was bright and curious. I never saw these as a means to an end, only as a way of broadening my knowledge and experience and a way to meet others in the field.

One board I joined was the GNVQ – the General National Vocational Qualification. The qualification has since been replaced by BTEC qualifications alongside other vocational qualifications, but at the time, its standard modules and exams were offered at Tamworth. Immediately, this gave me another insight into the delivery of GNVQ courses, the grading criteria, the resources associated with the qualification, as well as maintaining training standards to deliver it. Similarly, I sat on the board of City and Guilds, another professional qualification that is still offered throughout further education colleges.

My curiosity also took me into local industries with the purpose of forging relations between employers and the college. One placement I undertook was at Lloyds TSB. For a week, I shadowed staff in the bank's head office, learning how it operated, and most importantly, identifying ways that students taking vocational courses in finance and banking could benefit from the link. One large local employer at the time was a regional newspaper. My week there was a very memorable experience. Watching how raw copy, typed on a computer, was then edited and designed to seeing a final product roll off the presses was very impressive. I could not believe my eyes when I was taken into the print hall as reams of paper were fed into the industrial-sized presses, only to come out at the end of the conveyor belt as a fully printed, folded newspaper, ready to be sold.

The more I learned and the more I worked in further education, the more I realised what a poor relation to mainstream education vocational studies were considered to be. They were poorly funded and badly recognised. Yet, the college and the industries I was visiting had so much to offer, and I completely understood this vocational educational route, having taken it myself.

Of course, I had to fight to go to every meeting or conference that sat outside of my day job. My principal demanded to know what value it served other than my own self-development. I needed to demonstrate exactly what I was bringing back to the college and how my newfound knowledge and experience would benefit it. Naturally, I always had an answer. Whether I produced a document or just knocked on someone's door, I was always able to argue my case and persuade them why it was important that I went.

Before I knew it, I had been at Tamworth for six years. I felt I had learned everything I needed to, and it was time to move on. After a couple of attempts at interviews, I was appointed to Stafford College as assistant principal. During the two years I worked there, I led its Ofsted inspection preparations. As a result, the college gained good to outstanding grades throughout, a significant improvement. But in my heart, I wanted to push myself further. I had come so far in life that I could not stop now. Now, I saw myself as ready to apply for the job of a college principal – a role that would undoubtedly be a big step up for me but one that I was determined to fulfil.

In around 2003, I began sending out applications to colleges around the country. I did not mind where those colleges were, as I was willing to travel. Shankar was settled in Burton. Our children had long since left home, and they were forging their own careers, so I was freer to pursue my own goals. Although we had always been busy establishing ourselves in this new country, in truth, our lives have always revolved around our children and their upbringing. After completing her schooling at Moreton Hall, Shalini graduated in economics from the University of Essex. It is a delight to see her doing so well and making a name for herself in the financial world. Sheel joined Christchurch College in Oxford, where he studied politics, philosophy and economics. Although I wanted him to be an academic, he had his heart set on fashion and continues to design the latest and the best in ladies' fashion. Sneh graduated in medicine from the University of Edinburgh and qualified as an ophthalmic surgeon with flying colours. Rather than practising medicine, he has established himself in medical management and continues to excel in his career. It is gratifying for us to see that they are all doing well.

Back then, until I started to apply for the principal post, I had never truly felt the barrier of a glass ceiling. I had always been able to perform at interview and also move within establishments to more challenging roles by displaying my skill and drive. Now, it was a different story. Sometimes, it felt as if I was sending out applications into thin air. Some of my applications were not considered at all, and at first, I became very downhearted. 'Why am I not succeeding?' I thought. 'What is it about my CV that employers don't like? What is it about me they don't like?' On other occasions, I was invited for interview, but I was not offered the job. For some reason, I was not able to convince them I was the right person. Was it my manner? My forthrightness? It became very hard to tell.

Whether my Asian heritage played a part, I do not know. Certainly, there were hardly any Asian or black minority ethnic (BAME) college principals at the time, and this may have been a barrier. Whatever the reason, I was trapped in a bottleneck, and I began to contemplate giving up. I spoke of my frustration with my children, as I was looking for answers. 'Mum, you have to keep going,' they encouraged me. I listened to their advice, but the more colleges I applied to, the more I realised that a principal's role was probably a step too far. For example, in some interviews, I was asked if I had experience in property and estate management, financial management and data management. Because further education colleges are funded by central government but run as autonomous businesses, any principal's job involves management of all these different aspects of the college – not experience I had ever had – and I realised I needed a stepping stone.

When a job came up as deputy principal at New College Nottingham, it caught my eye. The college campus was large with around seven sites, and the job would fill the gaps in my experience. The current principal at Nottingham, Geoff Hall, had a fearsome reputation, but this did not put me off in the slightest. If anything, when colleagues at Tamworth and Stafford tried to dissuade me from applying, it only made me more curious.

'Do you know Geoff? You will not survive one moment with him,' they warned me when several took me out for lunch.

Apparently, staff did not last too long under Geoff. The question in my mind was not how I would survive with Geoff but how he would survive with me. I did not know anything about him, but I did not care either. For me, the role at New College Nottingham would be perfect. As it turned out, friends were right. Geoff was an imposing man – a known figure in the sector with a no-nonsense attitude. However, my interview with him went well. The college was due an Ofsted inspection, and I had exactly the blend of skills needed to prepare for it and improve standards.

From the outset, I was very clear with Geoff. I wanted the job for a couple of years, and then I would be applying for principal roles. If he was going to give me a hard time when that moment came, then it was better if he did not employ me. I got the job, but I was under no illusion that my appointment was made to get the college through Ofsted with flying colours, which I eventually did. This was not without issues. As much as I respected Geoff, he was a micromanager, and I had been used to working with relative autonomy so long as I produced the right results.

'The way our relationship is going, you and I are not going to last long together,' I said to him after my appointment. Politely but firmly, I told him that he had employed me to do a job, and I should be left to get on with it.

'Let me do the job I'm being paid to do,' I stressed to him. In all honesty, Geoff was not a natural when it came to people, and I could see that in dealing with external visitors to the college, he could easily make them uncomfortable. It was not the type of relationship-building the college needed.

To my surprise, Geoff agreed. From that day onwards, he did not interfere in my work. Moreover, once those boundaries had been established, I learned so much from Geoff. He was incredibly knowledgeable and had a thorough approach to analysing policy and all sorts of areas I had no clue about. I also found him to be a very fair man. He promoted the idea of gender equality and viewed social inclusion, particularly of minority groups, very positively. He believed that no matter where a person was from, people should be given the chance to succeed based on their abilities.

Openly, I was also pursuing my goal to be head of my own college, and Geoff was supporting me. In fact, he wrote many letters in support, and I sought advice from him on many occasions. When a principal's job came up at West Nottinghamshire College in Mansfield, he was the first person I approached to hear his opinion.

'Have you ever been to Mansfield, Asha?' he said.

'No,' I replied a little nervously.

'Mansfield is a difficult place,' he warned me before offering to drive me around. Mansfield was a poor community, he explained, an ex-mining area with substandard housing, several generations of worklessness and a poverty of aspiration.

'I don't want to be driven there,' I told him. In truth, my mind was already made up. This was the job I wanted. I did not want him to convince me otherwise. Whatever challenges I faced there, I was ready to throw myself into the role and make a real difference.

6
Champion of Change

'We cannot build the future for our youth, but we can build our youth for the future'

Franklin D Roosevelt

On the day I was offered the job at West Nottinghamshire College, I could barely sleep a wink. Going around in my mind were so many questions: what was I was going to do? How was I going to shape this role? How was I going to shape this college? This was the job I had been dreaming of for so long, yet now it was mine, the feeling was overwhelming.

It had not been long since my interview, and the anxiety of waiting for the outcome had got to me. For three days, I had been grilled by an expert panel, students and community groups. It felt like being dissected with a knife and fork, even though my vision had been clear – even more so when I stepped onto the campus in Mansfield for the very first time.

One of the first things I noticed was how lacking in aspiration the area seemed and how tired and grey the college buildings looked with their concrete exteriors and dated, shabby interiors. Naturally, the conversation with Geoff was fresh in my mind, and I had also done my homework. I knew that after the closure of the mining and textile industries, there was grinding unemployment throughout its mainly white working-class community. People needed something to reach for. Immediately, I looked to shaping a college that the community needed and deserved.

As part of the interview process, I had been required to present my vision. For me, it was easy. My inspiration came from the famous human rights activist Martin Luther King, 'I have a dream . . .' I began. 'I have a dream that the college will become a beacon of beacons, that it will put Mansfield on the world map, that aspirations will be raised and that together, we will achieve excellence'. In my heart, I wanted people to see what five star looked like. Occasionally, I jokingly elevated it to seven stars! It seemed to stick in the minds of staff because following one of my early staff inductions, I received an email from one teacher, Cheryl Fewkes, who wrote, 'You spoke with great passion and instilled in me self-belief that I can in fact make a difference at this college. Your presentation had a profound effect on me, and all the people in the room felt as inspired – you will see your five-star college a reality, an inspiration to the people of Mansfield'.

The college in its entirety was spread across five campuses catering for around 14,000 students and 1,000 staff. It was the second-largest employer in the area behind the NHS. Its main campus, at Derby Road, was just off a main junction on the outskirts of the town. In my mind, I saw it as a gateway – an institution that must look iconic, that was clearly defined as a place of learning and that oozed confidence. My motto then was, 'Good is not good enough,' and that stayed with me throughout my whole 12 years as principal and CEO.

Somehow, from the moment I arrived, I felt at home. 'I belong here,' I told myself. Even when I sat behind my desk in my new office for the first time, I knew that this was my college, my people, my job and my responsibility. It struck me that this was my first proper official leadership role, even though I had been a leader in my own right before then.

My first challenge was how I would go about embracing the students, the staff and the wider community. For this, I needed a strategic vision. Three pillars came to my mind: I wanted the college to be a dynamic institution for aspiring communities that achieved excellence. In setting this vision, I reminded myself of my own educational journey – I could barely believe that it was only three decades before when I had arrived in the UK with one suitcase, three children and no English whatsoever. My unconventional educational path led me to landing my first job at Oswestry College, and now it had taken me to the position of principal and CEO – exhilarating when I think about this now.

Not long afterwards, I rang the woman who was to become my long-term mentor, Jean Hardy, Chair of the College Board. Before coming to Mansfield,

I had not known Jean, who had been a human resource manager in the NHS. She had been the lead on the interview panel and supported my appointment. In part, this was controversial. The job had been earmarked for the incumbent deputy principal and me being awarded the job was not without some tension.

'What do you think of my vision?' I asked Jean a little nervously. Jean, an energetic and positive person, did not hesitate to give me her full backing.

'Go for it, Asha,' she said without skipping a beat. Just as she has done on so many subsequent occasions, Jean gave me confidence. At this juncture, my mission was to begin an ongoing conversation inside and outside of the college about how we were going to change our approach, our behaviour and our presentation in order to reach new heights. In all of my conversations, I was always careful to use the word 'we'. In my mind, this was a vision everyone had ownership of, and it could not be realised without their help and support.

Not everything was plain sailing. At first, resistance was there, and I learned quickly that not everyone wanted to embrace the changes I saw as necessary. Although my vision was obvious to me, I needed to work hard to sell it to the college's executive board to win the hearts and minds of my people.

Another challenge to overcome was that before my arrival, there had been a culture of board members not being free to discuss problems. I set out to change that. The only way that I, or the college, could address any issues was by encouraging transparency. I wanted staff to speak up when something was wrong, and I also wanted to ask my own searching questions of the board.

When I arrived, the college also had a planned financial deficit. To balance the books, I needed to create efficiencies, and this involved looking at all aspects of the college's running. I had to take some difficult decisions, and my intended changes made a lot of staff uncomfortable. There were some who were excited and shared my vision while others were happy with the status quo. However, there were a handful who decided to leave. To help me, I had to surround myself with a senior team I could trust, so a number of people who had worked with me in the past joined me. For example, this included a new finance director who, in fact, was a person my previous boss, Geoff Hall, had been trying to recruit to his own college for some time. When he heard about the appointment, Geoff rang me immediately.

‘What have you got that I haven’t got?’ he joked.

‘I’m more beautiful than you,’ I laughed, but in truth, I knew it was my passion, drive and ability to get things done that attracted new talent to the college. I was also keen to empower people to do their jobs and take ownership over their roles – the same chance to shape themselves that I had been given by Shaun McLaughlin and his deputy Ron Pugh at Oswestry College and that I had built for myself ever since.

From early on, I was also very fortunate to have the support of people within the wider community, including the local enterprise group, Mansfield 2020. However, this only happened after I presented my vision. To do this, I hired out the Civic Centre, which I did not necessarily expect to fill, but I aimed high. On the evening of my first speech, I was surprised to be standing in front of hundreds of faces. Far from the community lacking aspiration, parents, local business leaders and other notable people turned out to listen to me, and this began a long-term relationship between the college and the community.

Inside, I felt a real boost, and it spurred me on to develop further relationships. At the college, we had a fine-dining restaurant to train the students. So, I invited guests – for example, local employers, entrepreneurs and community leaders – for breakfasts, lunches and dinners. Vice-chancellors from regional universities also joined me. This gave me an opportunity to share my vision and build partnerships to achieve my goals.

Many who attended my presentations wrote kind words to me afterwards. At the college, Steve McAlone, Head of the Creative Arts Department, sent me a note following a stakeholder event at the Civic Centre. ‘I think a lot of people were stunned by the whole thing – you stole the show. Your passion, commitment, enthusiasm, drive and humour shone. You were inspirational; it was a privilege to witness it,’ he wrote. In a letter following a breakfast meeting from the then-Mansfield 2020 chairman, Irvin Robinson, he called the passion and enthusiasm with which I was driving the college forward ‘infectious’. He also recognised that tackling the worklessness agenda through partnerships with local businesses, schools, colleges and other agencies was an important one, and he gave me the full support of Mansfield 2020.

Likewise, when I invited John Sankey MBE, a senior community leader, to meet with numerous employers in the area, he likened me to a 'whirlwind'. He added, 'When strangers speak so highly of you, I know exactly what you are achieving'. These comments, in particular, meant a lot to me.

The partnerships I forged with the area's business community became invaluable. One programme at the college I set out to grow was that of apprenticeships. The 'earn as you learn' model was perfect for a vocational college such as West Nottinghamshire, yet on my arrival, few people knew who the big employers in the area were, and those same employers did not know what the college had to offer in terms of training.

One large printing firm in Mansfield had a multi-million pound turnover, yet we were not sending any of our 150 apprentices there. Then, there was the holiday company Centre Parcs with whom the college did have a relationship, but one that had not been nurtured over time. Immediately, I set out to change the perception of our programme and re-engage with employers. Over the next months and years, I also developed relationships with the crème de la crème of British business, including engineering firms such as Jaguar and Land Rover, increasing our apprenticeship programme to 14,000 students at its peak. To raise the profile and importance of vocational training further, I also introduced an apprenticeship award ceremony to be held at the House of Lords. This became an annual event attended by apprentices, their parents and employers. Again, it was humbling for me to witness the pride and joy on the faces of the apprentices and their parents, some of whom had never been to London before, let alone the House of Lords.

Similarly, links were also forged with local councils. One project involved students creating art for Mansfield Civic Centre. Another joint initiative involved taking courses out from the college and into local communities. This programme offered courses in subjects from arts to IT, accessible to people unreachable in the community, and it encouraged lifelong learning – in exactly the same way I had benefited from by taking my typing course.

I also reinstated A-levels. Previously, courses had been available to students, but due to declining exam grades, the syllabus had been withdrawn. I asked a question: how could we do justice to students if we restricted what academic options were available to them? Again, just as I had been given the right to reach my potential, I wanted to pass this on. It was not an easy task, but it became a rewarding one. For example, two years later, one of our A-level students was admitted to Cambridge University to study natural sciences. She went on to receive a first-class honours degree. Only a few years earlier, that would have been an impossible thought at West Nottinghamshire College.

One year after my appointment, I travelled to India and met with senior government officials there. During my brief visit, I wanted to develop links between West Nottinghamshire College and the wider world. Naturally, India was close to my heart, but I also saw an opportunity to forge links with its burgeoning economic powerhouses and those industries that would benefit from an exchange of vocational skills.

I cannot remember exactly how the meeting came about, but when I learned I was to meet one of India's most renowned educators, it almost took my breath away. I had long admired Dr APJ Abdul Kalam, the then-President of India and a true visionary. From his own humble village background in Tamil Nadu, he had risen to become a space scientist and had gone on to serve one term as president before returning to his civilian life of education, writing and public service.

As I walked through the entrance of the famous Rashtrapati Bhavan in Delhi, I did so with a sense of utter disbelief. Was I really going to meet this man who had been a hero of mine – and a hero of India – for so long? Flanked by two bodyguards clasping rifles, I was escorted through the historical corridors to the President's main office. When I took my seat opposite him, I was even more taken aback. Dr Abdul Kalam, an animated and resolute man, knew all about the college. When I told him about my life and how I had travelled from Bihar to Britain, he replied as if he had met me before – he knew so much about me.

Jean Hardy MBE also accompanied me, and during our hour-long conversation, I listened to him intently, becoming more and more mesmerised by what an inspirational and deep thinker he was. His vision about igniting the minds of children and putting the future in their hands sent shivers down my spine. He talked so eloquently about how each individual can make a difference if they are shown the way.

'If we teach people to evolve and shape their lives, then one day their next page will be to shape the nation. And you, Asha, will be remembered for writing that page, whether it is a page of discovery or of fighting injustice,' he told me.

Then, he paused and leaned over before quietly asking, 'So, Asha, what will be your page in the book of life?'

I was momentarily speechless before I could gather my thoughts. Eventually, I replied, 'Sir, my page is the page of learning. I have been learning about myself and the world around me. Every day is a learning day for me.'

'Do you ever teach in the classroom?' he asked.

I admitted that since leaving my role as a lecturer, I had not. At that, he leaned in again and offered me a few words more.

'Never lose sight of the route you came from. Go back into the classroom and teach,' he said, before we parted company.

When I rang Shankar that evening, I was bubbling over with excitement, and when I boarded my flight back to England, the words of Dr Abdul Kalam were still ringing in my ears. From that day onwards, I made a point of going back into the classroom to teach leadership skills as well as running the college. My speeches went down well with students, and I always made sure to take them on delegations with me.

From the moment I started at the college, I also never made myself unapproachable to any person. Whereas before when even the administrative corridors had been out of bounds, my door was always open. I picked up litter in the corridors, and I spoke to everyone – from the deputy principal to the cleaning staff. In fact, when I saw cleaning staff in the corridors, I always asked how they were and often invited them to have a coffee with me in my office. There, they could share some of the issues they faced, such as the mess they always found in the ladies' toilets. When my monthly meeting with students rolled around, I raised these concerns. 'For the first time, we feel we are being treated as equals in the college. Before you came, we were just cleaners,' the cleaners told me afterwards when the problem was resolved. It was important to me that staff felt valued. Every time I spoke to them, either in groups or individually, my message was that each and every one was making a contribution to the organisation, and everyone was important.

One year, when we had a financial surplus, we decided to use it to reward staff with a bonus, so we gave everyone the same amount regardless of their position. This gesture generated a lot of goodwill and happiness among the workforce, which I always felt was necessary in our pursuit of excellence. As far as staff were concerned, I always wanted to inspire them, and given much of their feedback, I believe I was able to achieve this. Following one of the principal's breakfasts I hosted, Tammy Penford, a senior member of staff for learners with mental health difficulties, said how lovely it was to meet me in a less formal setting. 'I think it's great that you make yourself so accessible to staff and learners,' she wrote. Likewise, the 'skills for life' tutor, Kirsty Stevens, said I had made her feel inspired to lead in her role. 'You encouraged me to feel empowered,' she wrote. That my staff's ideas were being discussed and taken seriously also did not go unnoticed. The early years tutor, Lesley Henstock, told me how motivating this was and how delighted she was to see an outcome to some of her proposals.

I also made a point of sitting in the canteen on occasion to eat with students. I never wanted to be an untouchable leader, and I understood that my visibility was important. More than that, I also loved talking to them.

'Your make-up is always perfect, Mrs Khemka,' I remember one student saying to me, before asking me where I bought it from.

'Boots, just like you,' I laughed. Although exchanges like this seemed insignificant, I felt it mattered that the students could talk to me like that.

At other, more formal lunch meetings with them, I was always keen to hear about their ambitions, and I tried to help them achieve their goals. I remember one student, Josh, who had taken A-levels at the college. 'Before I met you, I had never thought of applying to Oxford,' he said, adding that he really wanted to study law but that he needed work experience at a law firm for his application to be taken seriously. Hearing this was music to my ears, as I was able to arrange a placement for him at the law firm Eversheds.

Outside the college, I also never missed an opportunity to highlight our work and the life-enhancing opportunities the college could give. One time, I was in a taxi moving from one campus to another when I got chatting to the driver. 'Where did you study?' I asked him. He explained that he had never had the chance to go onto further education, as he had had to work. His parents had wanted him to get a job, even though they did not work themselves.

'You can do both!' I told him enthusiastically, before reeling off a list of part-time and evening courses that he could fit in around his driving. Of course, I told him about my own journey and how I had run a home, taken care of my family and studied at the same time. How gratifying it was that a week or so later, when I was in the college foyer, I noticed the exact same man chatting to the receptionist while a tutor helped him choose a course. It was amazing for me – and so touching – that such a small conversation like that could change someone's future direction.

Alongside enhancing the apprenticeship programme and widening the curriculum on offer, my next goal was to find a way to overhaul the building structure of the college, which was so badly needed. Every time I arrived at work, I was struck by the college's exterior, which looked like a 1960s eyesore crying out for attention. As I walked through the corridors, I felt energy sapping from me. My dream had been to create a 'super centre' – a statement that West Nottinghamshire College meant business, that we were not taking no for an answer and that we would be in the heart of the community for years to come.

However, this road also had many obstacles. At the time, we looked at funding the building through grants available from central government, and we also looked to our own balance sheet. After starting in my role, the college's deficit had turned around, and many of its assets had started to earn money. For example, the college owned an e-learning business called BKSB, an online software tool to teach maths and English, which we sold on licence to schools and other colleges around the country. Our income from it increased from £500,000 to more than £5m.

At first, we were able to progress the building project with £70m of funding pledged to us by the then-Learning and Skills Council (LSC), as it was undergoing a programme to fund the refurbishing of more than 150 further education colleges around the country. Locally, we also had growing support from planning chiefs who had given us the go-ahead to push on with plans to sell our main site and move to a new base with a state-of-the-art facility to be built by 2010. The benefit of this was that most teaching could be carried out from one location. The plans also included provision for a theatre, a new fine-dining restaurant, a new sports hall and a technology park that would allow the college to thrive.

Although I was fully aware of the hurdles, I also sensed a real buzz of excitement around the college. Within the community too, there was a feeling that something was happening and that the area was finally being put on the map. The college was also attracting much media attention, and I loved every moment of being at the centre of it. I had an overwhelming sense of fulfilment that the vision I had had in my mind from the first day I stepped into the college grounds was finally being recognised. Personally, I felt energised. I made the college my life, even though this did not happen without me making many compromises. Long hours, combined with coming home late to my household duties, – alongside juggling other priorities – meant that I had almost forgotten what a social life even looked like!

What I had not predicted was the devastating news that was to follow. During 2008, I received a call telling me that the funding pledged by the LSC could no longer be honoured. A black hole of £2.7bn had been found in the LSC's own accounts, and much of its rebuilding programme was to be terminated. For me personally, this was one of the biggest setbacks I had ever experienced. It hit my stomach like the weight of a bowling ball. Of course, it was also a huge blow to the college, and I had the terrible task of breaking the news to everyone who had worked so hard on the project. Collectively, it was as if the rug had been pulled from under our feet.

In that moment, I probably learned more about leadership than at any other time. It is all well and good to take the glory when great things happen, but I also had to take responsibility when setbacks occurred. With architects already on board and planning permission almost granted, we had not expected to go back to square one at such a late stage. However, this was our reality. Now, people were looking to me for answers.

Over the next few months, we re-analysed. Instead of rebuilding in one go, we scaled back plans and looked to refurbish sites stage by stage. Given that the college finances were healthy, we were able to secure a bank loan to partially cover the costs. It was not a compromise I ever wanted to face, but it was the only way we could deliver on our promise.

Fortunately, that year was a success in so many other ways. At the start of 2008, I had news that Ofsted were to inspect the college for the first time in four years. Having previously been part of the Ofsted process, I knew how rigorous the assessment would be and how I would have to prepare my staff for the visit. Over the course of a week, 15 inspectors combed through every aspect of the college's workings. From its finance to its quality of teaching, to its outside partnerships to its governance, interviews took place with staff, students and outside employers, to name a few.

Admittedly, it was a tense moment. The last inspection before my appointment had delivered a 'good' ranking. Naturally, the outcome of this visit would not just be a judgement on the college but of my leadership in the two years since becoming principal. Although I had made many friends within the college by now, alongside inroads throughout the community and beyond, I felt that so much rested on the result.

To this day, I will never forget the anxious wait before receiving the news that we had achieved 'outstanding' status in all key areas. In fact, this still makes me emotional with pride. Within the report, which was published that summer, inspectors praised the college for its excellence in governance and financial management. It also highlighted the 'powerful partnerships' we had created, our impressive track record on student success and our 'imaginative and innovative approaches' to ensuring local people engaged with learning. The leadership of the college was also cited as outstanding.

Wow! For me, this moment encapsulated everything I had been aiming for. Education had been my silver bullet. It had been a way for me to spread my wings and fly – to grow in self-confidence and to prepare myself for the world of work. To know that I was doing the same for others and delivering a high-quality experience gave me a great deal of fulfilment.

That year, two of our students were interviewed by the local paper in Mansfield, and both had their own remarkable educational journeys to share. One 18-year-old called James had been held back by a visual impairment, yet he had passed his A-level media and AS-level business and law exams. Another student, Karen, who was 43 and had been out of work for several years, had felt so underconfident about learning again that she took her husband to the first session of her word-processing course. Both students had gone on to study for an honours degree. Stories like this meant everything to me, especially given that Mansfield was – and continues to be – a place with many challenges to overcome.

Just how many challenges there were was evident from the many students and parents I talked to. Of course, we also catered for children with learning difficulties, among other impairments. When it came to children who needed specialist care, I am reminded of one parent who approached me during an awards ceremony moments after I had made my speech. 'I feel privileged to be shaking your hand,' she told me. Her son had multiple learning difficulties, and she explained that attending the college had given him confidence and an opportunity he never would have had. 'He looks forward to coming to the college. He enjoys his time here, and I can't wait until he goes onstage to receive an award from you,' she continued. What an emotional and gratifying experience that was.

Ofsted inspectors had also been impressed with our future building plans which, at the time of the inspection, looked set to go ahead. Of course, that remained a source of disappointment after funding was withdrawn. Nevertheless, with a loan secured and a revised plan underway, we were able to make a start. One of these projects was realised early on in 2009 when we unveiled the new £7.2m Construction and Logistics Skills Academy. The new facility, designed for 600 students, was formed from an industrial shell and spread across several floors, each representing a step up the qualification ladder. With courses in bricklaying, plumbing, carpentry, gas fitting, painting and decorating, forklift truck driving and railway engineering among others, it became our flagship Station Park Academy.

What made the launch of the site particularly special was that HRH Prince of Wales came to unveil it. The visit happened after two local councillors contacted him, highlighting the problem of education in the area. Somehow, at Clarence House, they had remembered the letter, and when Prince Charles heard of the new facility, he requested a visit. For weeks beforehand, we prepared. Then, days before we were due to roll out the red carpet for His Royal Highness, I was locked in meetings with his staff, running through the security detail. I had never seen so many sniffer dogs and bodyguards combing every corner of the building, but given that it was the first ever visit by a royal to the college, I knew it was necessary.

When Prince Charles arrived at the college, the Lord-Lieutenant of Nottinghamshire Sir Andrew Buchanan introduced us, and as Prince Charles shook my hand, I extended my special welcome to him. As I guided him around, he met stakeholders, community leaders and strategic partners. I was surprised to see that he seemed to know a few people already, including the founder of the Purico Group and one of Nottinghamshire's most successful entrepreneurs, Nathu Puri.

'Good to see you, Nat. How are you doing?' the prince said.

He also shared some light-hearted conversations with Nick Linney, the chairman of the Mansfield-based print company that the college had built such close ties with. As it turned out, both men had gone to the same school – Gordonstoun in Scotland.

Shankar, Sheel and Shalini were also there to receive the prince. The only person missing was Sneh, who was travelling abroad for work.

'What do you do?' Prince Charles asked Shankar when they shook hands.

'Your Highness, I'm an orthopaedic surgeon,' he said.

'Where did you qualify from?' Prince Charles continued.

'I studied in Patna at the Prince of Wales Medical College'.

Suddenly, Prince Charles seemed a little bothered.

'I understand they have changed the name of the medical college now. Do you know why they did that?' he asked Shankar.

'You probably know better than I do!' Shankar replied politely.

When it came to Sheel's turn to answer the prince's question about what he did for a living, he replied, 'I am a ladies' fashion designer.'

'Do you know, I've always wanted to do that!' the prince laughed.

When Shalini explained that she worked at LDC on investment deals in London, he smiled and whispered to her, 'I have brought my portrait which your mum asked for, but don't tell her, so I can surprise her later'.

'Where is your other brother? I don't see him here,' the prince then asked Shalini.

'Sir, he has sent his apology. He couldn't come. He's speaking at a conference in Belgium,' she said.

'What is he speaking about?'

'He's speaking about health. He is an ophthalmic surgeon,' Shalini replied with her usual charm and smile.

'That's good. Please give him my best wishes. Tell him that I missed him,' he said, before moving to the next guests.

Then, we moved to the curriculum areas, where the students were working on many of the trade disciplines the college offered. The prince seemed impressed and commented on how we were skilling young people with state-of-the-art equipment that he had seen in modern industry. As we passed from area to area, quite a few of the students crowded onto the balconies in the central area to take photographs. They were so excited to send messages to their parents and friends to tell them that they were meeting the future king. Prince Charles then stopped to speak to some of the students about what they were doing, what they enjoyed and what they planned for the future. One young man he exchanged a few words with was working with his plumbing tools, but it just so happened that he looked very much like Prince Harry. It was a detail the newspapers picked up on. When a report featured in *The Mirror* the next day, there was a picture of the prince talking to our Harry lookalike.

Prince Charles was even given the opportunity to show off his artistic side by creating marble-style patterns using a feather on a canvas as part of the painting and decorating course. Initially, I could see that he was hesitant.

'Go on. Give it a go,' I encouraged him.

'Don't you start,' he replied jokingly, but he did it and in the end did rather a good job.

'We're building a new engineering centre,' I explained as we walked around further. 'Will you come back to open it?'

'I'll only come if it's built with brick,' he replied, smiling. The prince is well known for being a traditionalist when it comes to architecture.

The visit itself generated much positive press. Although I did not feel it, one of my staff commented afterwards that for the first time ever, I looked nervous when I gave my welcome speech, but I figured I was only human. The only thing I remember about it was that Prince Charles seemed very attentive to what I had to say.

After that, the presence of dignitaries arriving at the college only increased and not just from the UK. From the outset, I had wanted to create an international strategy and build relationships with other countries, and my aforementioned trip to India had been part of this. The Indian High Commissioner, His Excellency Mr Ranjan Mathai, arrived to see the college's engineering and training facilities, and he commented that they were the best he had ever seen. For me, persuading an Indian dignitary to visit was a real coup – never seen before at a UK FE college!

Similarly, I was also building ties in Eastern Europe. For example, the Bulgarian ambassador visited the college to meet with BTEC travel and tourism students, following a staff exchange to the Bulgarian skiing resort of Momchilgrad the previous year.

When I look back now, those first few years at West Nottinghamshire College were like riding a rollercoaster. I am not sure now how I was able to juggle everything, but I know much of my drive came from being part of a college that was succeeding. Of course, no matter what disappointments we had to overcome, I always had the support of Shankar and my children.

At home, our own renovation project was underway, but it would be many, many years before we would realise our vision given how busy both Shankar and I were with our careers. The house we had finally bought in Burton-on-Trent had been a dream of ours for some time. A former country house hotel on a stretch of beautiful rolling countryside, it was a proper English manor house. During the period when we were housed in hospital accommodation, Shankar and I often drove past it and dreamed about seeing a 'for sale' sign outside. When that did happen, we jumped at the chance to buy it whatever the price, even though it was Grade II-listed and we had underestimated how much work was needed on it. The flowery interior was not exactly to our taste when we first stepped inside, but immediately, I sensed it was a place of happiness. As a hotel, it had been used for weddings and honeymoons, and now it was to become our home sweet home.

While I got to grips with my new role during the day, I came home to brick dust at night. Builders were constantly trooping in and out of the front door. At one point, our children even suggested to us that it would be better if we just sold the house and moved, such was the chaos we were living in, but Shankar and I had fallen in love, and we were not ready to have our hearts broken.

With this house and the college blossoming, I was also starting to enjoy some personal recognition. Given the educational and career route I had taken so late in life, this meant everything to me. Not long after I began at the college, I was one of only two Asian women principals in Britain. That the college was now in the top 5% for its success rates had not gone unnoticed, and in the summer of 2007, I was honoured to receive the Jewel Award at a ceremony in Birmingham sponsored by Lloyds TSB. In winning the category in healthcare and education, I wanted the award to shine like a beacon to other women, particularly women from black or ethnic minority backgrounds seeking promotion in education.

Likewise, a year later, I won the Asian Woman of Achievement Award, and the story was covered in both the UK and India. The ceremony, held in London at London's Park Lane Hilton, was attended by Prime Minister Tony Blair's wife Cherie and a number of other dignitaries, including Hollywood star Liz Hurley, the famous British actress and model. Afterwards, I reiterated the words that I always told my students: with courage and determination, ambition and drive to do something – then it can be done. In fact, whenever I was interviewed, I always thought back to the plaque on my wall in my office emblazoned with the words of Abraham Lincoln.

But by far the greatest honour of my early career at West Nottinghamshire College came in November 2009. Then, I had been driving home on a dark and foggy evening when Shankar called me. 'How long will you be?' he said excitedly. A surprise was waiting for me, he explained, but he refused to say what. For the next hour or so, anxiety pulsed through me as I tried to keep a steady hand on the steering wheel. The minute I arrived home, he was waiting. 'Here,' he said, grinning as he handed me a letter stamped with the insignia of the Cabinet Office. When I opened the letter, a deep sense of fulfilment spread over me. I had been nominated for an OBE (Officer of the Order of the British Empire) and been invited to attend Buckingham Palace in the new year to receive the honour. For six weeks, I had to keep it a secret. Only Shankar and the children knew about it until my name was announced in the New Year's Honours list.

Naturally, I was thrilled to receive many heartfelt messages of congratulations. One in particular that stood out was from Nick Linney. He wrote, 'For us old-timers who have been here for generations, we see people come and go and are usually disappointed, especially in local government and education. You are different. I'd like you to stay as long as you possibly can'. Certainly, I had poured my heart and soul into West Nottinghamshire College, and his words resonated with me.

Six months later, Shankar, Shalini, Sheel and Sneh all joined me as I received my award. Instead of wearing a sari, I chose a Chanel jacket with pearl fastenings that looked almost military in style and which brought together my Indian heritage and my recognition of how England had shaped me.

'How long have you been at the college?' the Queen enquired when we met. It was the first time I had been introduced to Her Majesty the Queen, and I was completely spellbound to stand in front of her in the most opulent of surroundings of the Grand Room at Buckingham Palace. I had to remind myself that it had only been three years since my appointment at West Nottinghamshire College, yet so much had been achieved. As I curtsied in front of her and she pinned the red sash and gold cross on my heart, I thought about growing up in India. There, I would never have dared to dream I could embark upon such a breath-taking journey.

Afterwards, Shalini had organised a surprise celebration, and I was taken to a large room on the roof of the Hilton Park Lane Hotel in London, where many of our close friends were awaiting my arrival. As I turned and saw the assembled crowd, a lump formed in my throat, and tears welled up in my eyes. My children had gone to such great efforts to organise the event. Receiving an OBE is one thing, but experiencing the love and affection of your children is the most precious gift in life!

With His Excellency Dr Abdul Kalam, President of India, at the president's house in New Delhi in 2007

Receiving the 'Asian woman of achievement', award presented by Cherie Blair in London in 2008

Receiving the NRI Gold award from the Indian High Commissioner, His Excellency Nalin Surie and other Indian prominent leaders at the House of Lords in 2010

Welcoming His Royal Highness the Prince of Wales at my college in 2009

His Royal Highness the Prince of Wales in conversation with my family during his visit to my college in 2009

Receiving my OBE from Her Majesty the Queen at Buckingham Palace at the investiture ceremony in 2009

In the courtyard of Buckingham Palace following my OBE investiture in 2009

With my family after receiving my OBE at Buckingham Palace in 2009

Receiving a bouquet with fond blessings from one of the closest friends of my father at a reception organised by my uncles in Sitamarhi to mark my OBE and home coming in 2010

Welcoming His Royal Highness the Duke of Kent at the opening ceremony of the Arts Centre of my college in 2011

In conversation with the British Prime Minister the Right Honourable Gordon Brown at number 10 Downing Street in 2010

7

Shaping Education

'I slept and dreamt that life was joy. I awoke and saw that life was service. I acted and behold, service was joy'

Rabindranath Tagore

At West Nottinghamshire College, my hunger for knowledge and influence did not stop when I took over. In fact, it only intensified. After finding my feet in the first couple of years, I knew I could spread my wings a little further and become a powerful voice and a useful advocate for my sector. Although perceptions are now slowly changing, the further education sector has always been seen as the poor relation when compared to schools and universities. When I became principal and CEO, it remained badly funded and little understood by others, in particular by government. Yet, the transformation I was experiencing on the ground painted an altogether different picture. The energy and dynamism that permeated through every corridor in the college was electric. I was witnessing on a day-to-day basis an unlocking of talent that many students never knew they had.

For this reason, I even changed the venue for our graduation ceremonies. In previous years, the annual celebration had been held at Mansfield Civic Centre – a nice enough building but rather functional and lacking in atmosphere. I wanted students not just to achieve outstanding results but also to feel outstanding when they did so. After all, getting a degree is a high point in anyone's career, and it should be celebrated in inspiring surroundings. For this reason, Kelham Hall in Newark, a beautiful, gothic-style, Grade I-listed building set in acres of lush parkland, became the college's new graduation home. Our ceremonies took place in the great hall under its dramatic flying archway. Students attended alongside their families and friends, and I could feel everyone's emotion and pride as they walked onto the stage to receive their degree. For me, it was also a moment of immense joy to hand over their certificates. Before I delivered my address, I always thought about my own graduation journey from Cardiff University not that long ago. In many ways, I still felt like one of the students, and in my speeches, I often used examples of how people all over the world study against all the odds and go on to achieve great things in life.

One of the stories I shared was of a young boy called KR Narayanan, who was one of seven children in his family. Although he walked around 15 kilometres daily through paddy fields to get to school, he could not pay for his schooling. Instead, he listened to the lessons by standing outside of the classroom, and he borrowed books from other students and copied lessons down. In the end, not only did he obtain his BA and MA from the University of Kerala, but he was also awarded a Tata Scholarship to study politics, economics and journalism at the London School of Economics. Who could have predicted that one day he would become the first Dalit president of India, coming from people often known as 'untouchables,' who exist at the bottom of the ladder within India's caste system?

The graduation ceremony was also addressed by academics, vice-chancellors and other inspirational figures from political and business backgrounds – for example, Baroness Usha Prashar CBE and Lord Karan Bilimoria CBE.

On other occasions, I brought in key figures to the college who reiterated the message of 'aim high and you will get there'. Gold-medal-winning Olympian Dame Jessica Ennis-Hill enthralled the students with a speech about Olympian values. Meanwhile, entrepreneur Karen Brady CBE delivered a masterclass in starting a business. Founder of the Games Workshop Ian Livingstone OBE also delivered a masterclass for our computer science students. Living, breathing success stories gave students a chance to dream big – and role models to look up to.

Students also became part of the performance of the ceremony, in particular a young man called Christopher who had been pointed out to me previously by one of the music lecturers. 'I know you would like to meet him,' the lecturer said after he came to my office to explain how this student showed signs of excelling in music. When Christopher did come, he was suited and booted, but I sensed he was shy and nervous. Nevertheless, we talked, and he told me about his aspirations and how he would like to follow a musical career. Later, when I saw him play a couple of times, I realised just how good this young man actually was. 'Would you like to play the piano at our higher education graduation ceremony?' I asked. Immediately, I saw his eyes sparkle.

Although we had to go to the effort of transporting a piano to Kelham Hall, I was determined that this man would take centre stage and play a couple of pieces during each graduation session break. He did, and very special it was, too – not something you would see at other graduation ceremonies. When we broke for refreshments, I invited Chris to join me and the other staff, where I was able to get to know him a little better. In the end, Chris playing piano during our graduation ceremonies became an annual event, and I watched as he transformed from the shy boy I had met in my office to a confident man, stepping onto the stage with a firm footing. When he himself graduated with his music qualifications, he strode towards me to receive his degree, and I felt such inner joy to see this promising future star.

Over the years, I have kept in touch with Chris, and he has always kept me informed of what he is doing with his life. I am pleased to say he is now making his own records, and he tells me he has thousands of followers on Instagram. Not long ago, when he came to visit Shankar and me at home, he even took Shankar to a music shop in Mansfield and advised him which piano to buy after Shankar expressed an interest in learning the instrument following his retirement. Shankar is still considering whether to spend the cash!

Putting West Nottinghamshire College on the map was not only about raising local aspirations. Regionally, it was just as important to highlight the work of my college but also all the further education colleges in the area. After all, each of us were experiencing the same challenges. By sharing knowledge, expertise and developing forward-thinking strategies together, this allowed us to further deliver and inspire. From early on, I had even mooted the idea of a federation of colleges grouped together under a single vision and strategic direction across region or sub-region. That way, colleges could remain autonomous yet develop their own specialisms. An umbrella organisation would enable us to engage in more meaningful ways with regional development agencies, local authorities and central government to create efficiencies and unlock funding that could then be ploughed back into learning. That is a larger vision that has yet to be realised but one that I think still holds merit. Whichever way, we needed policymakers to know that collectively we had power, we could make a difference, and our voices needed to be heard.

One organisation that I became involved with was the Association of Colleges (AoC) – a member organisation that provided advocacy for FE colleges. In 2009, when I first began sitting on the AoC board, the prevailing feeling was that the further education sector was not being promoted in the way other sectors were. Yet, at the same time, we were also acutely aware that the UK had a worsening skills shortage, especially in employment areas, such as engineering and construction, where we knew we could plug vital gaps.

Given that the country was still experiencing the shockwaves of the global financial crisis and was mired in a recession, it was obvious that we could make a real difference to a market in recovery. As the economy was set to grow, any future investment needed a skilled workforce to draw on. So, as well as looking at how colleges should be prioritised and funded better, what a common inspection framework for Ofsted should look like, what our rights were and so on, we also wanted to send a clear message, 'We are a vital lynchpin in a recovering economy, and we are big businesses in our own rights'. And West Nottinghamshire College *was* a big business and one that was starting to be recognised as such.

I had been exceptionally proud that after 2008 and our 'outstanding' Ofsted report, my college had been held up as an exemplar of a great business. Not long afterwards, it was similarly hailed as a first-class employer, having been awarded star status by the accreditation firm Best Companies, which assessed the college not only on its leadership but also on other criteria such as relationships between staff and managers alongside personal wellbeing. The college also appeared at number 14 on *The Sunday Times'* best 75 places to work in the public sector list, giving it a real boost. Likewise, to be recognised as one of the top five CEOs in the country for leadership was a great personal boost for myself.

Scooping the education 'Oscar' also meant so much to me. In 2009, we received 'Beacon Status' from the Learning and Skills Improvement Service. In recognition of the outstanding running of the college and the quality of teaching provided, we had now been placed among the top-performing colleges in the country. I had always wanted the college to become a beacon of beacons, but this was the icing on the cake. When it actually happened, it only gave me more energy to strive for even greater success. As a Beacon Status college, we were also required to work with the Learning and Skills Council to share our expertise and good practice with the rest of the sector and help drive up performance nationwide.

With student numbers at the college now reaching around 25,000 and it being nationally recognised, I felt I had the platform to become an even more forceful advocate. Driving home the message of what the sector could offer and the challenges it faced came naturally to me. The college was my life, not just a job, and I was able to harness that passion. As I put myself forward for more roles, more opportunities also came my way: people invited me either to chair boards or become a participating member of them.

I also began speaking publicly about the variety of issues that we were facing on a regular basis. For example, after a major shake-up in 2010, the Learning and Skills Council was abolished and replaced by the Skills Funding Agency and the Young People's Learning Agency, but the transition had been rocky. Back then, public expenditure was being cut, and I wanted to make sure that my college and others did not bear the brunt of this. We all wanted to deliver first-class education to students, but without adequate resources, this was always made harder. Fresh in my mind was also the devastating impact that budget cuts had initially inflicted on our capital spending project – our proposed 'super-centre'.

Likewise, also on the agenda was the problem of NEETS – the teenagers who were neither in education nor employment or training. Sadly, in an area where former industries had given way to generations of worklessness, Mansfield suffered acutely from this problem. Despite countless government promises to do more to help jobless young people, the reality was different.

Tackling the problem by being a voice to influence government became a personal obsession of mine, and it still is. If we ever had a hope of engaging students in vocational training, then it was not just about welcoming them in, putting them on a course and hoping for the best. These students had difficult home circumstances and specific challenges. Some had been in trouble with the police; others had problems with drugs and alcohol or had suffered bullying or domestic abuse. Others had caring responsibilities at home, which prevented them from attending school. Giving them the right support and nurturing was key, but all that came at a high resource cost – resources that were constantly and frustratingly being squeezed.

Quite how much nurturing these children required needed to be seen to be believed. Words like, 'You're doing a great job,' were often met with hysterical laughter or complete disbelief. Some children had simply never been praised like that or told they were good before. They had little self-confidence at home, at school or anywhere else. They needed to be persuaded to develop self-belief and see a positive future in front of them. Perhaps my 20 years as a stay-at-home mother equipped me well to understand that students needed a holistic package of support if they had any chance of thriving.

Yet, all the time, I could see dizzying potential surrounding me. In many ways, this fed my constant enthusiasm to champion vocational education, which I did at many high-profile events, such as *The Sunday Times* Festival of Education in 2012. There, in a keynote address, I spoke about inspiring young people through engagement, employability and links with enterprise. Potential not only surrounded me in the college but in every business in Mansfield and beyond, and where we were located made us central to a potential economic powerhouse. In particular, the Midlands' focus was on engineering and manufacturing, and so, I was invited to sit on several regional boards aimed at developing a strategic vision for the region as an engine for growth.

A few years later, I was asked to represent FE colleges on the Local Enterprise Partnership Board, which spanned Derbyshire and Nottinghamshire. This also gave me a fascinating insight into shaping regional strategy, and I was always keen to keep my finger on the pulse of opportunities and change. For example, we developed a vision for 2030 that the region would be a world-class, innovation-led, highly productive economy with a global reputation for manufacturing excellence. Naturally, colleges would be pivotal in creating world-class education, a training system and a well-qualified workforce able to fully participate in the economy and share in its benefits.

Gradually, as I raised the college's profile, I also had the ear of government ministers who I made sure to invite to the college to showcase how we were shaping the future. Among the many who visited over the years to witness what we had achieved were Geoff Hoon MP, the Defence Secretary; Mark Spencer MP, currently the Chief Whip; Justine Greening MP, the Education Secretary; Matthew Hancock MP, Skills Minister; and Sir Alan Meale, the longstanding MP for Mansfield.

Jeremy Corbyn, the Labour leader, even requested a visit. That happened just before the 2017 general election when the party were fighting for the Mansfield seat – a traditional Labour heartland. On that occasion, he had wanted to engage with young people, and I had the pleasure of having an audience with him one to one.

'Why did you choose to come to the college?' I asked him.

He smiled and replied rather affectionately, 'I have heard a lot about the college and about the work you have done here. You are the best'. I felt like that was a genuine remark, and he meant what he said.

When he was about to go downstairs to address the 500 or so people waiting to hear him speak, the photographer signalled for us to have our photograph taken. Suddenly, I watched as Mr Corbyn breathed in and adjusted his shirt, which had been loosely tucked into his trousers. Then, I noticed him straighten up his jacket to make himself look a bit more polished. 'You are very smartly dressed for the occasion,' he said, turning to look at me as he did so.

In fact, Jeremy Corbyn's speech went down very well, and he received a warm response. As he was departing, I wished him good luck for the forthcoming election and invited him to visit again. 'Definitely. It would be my honour,' he called back, but I never did see him. For the first time in 94 years, Labour lost its Mansfield seat, and instead, I welcomed the area's new MP called Ben Bradley, who I found to be sincere and engaging. Following his visits, students often commented that they liked what he had to say because he was young and fresh, and they could relate to him.

As I became a more forceful spokesperson and influencer, I was also stretching my own capabilities. If I could make a difference for my college, my community and for many others facing similar challenges, then I was happy, but I did not want to limit myself. After all, the UK had given me life-enriching opportunities, and I wanted to share my journey. On the occasions when the Department of Education asked me to speak at a variety of events, I spoke passionately about education being a 'right'. I was fortunate enough to have had the support to claim that right, but more needed to be done to encourage those who did not.

In particular, I saw the apprenticeship route as playing a key role, which is one reason why West Nottinghamshire College became one of the largest providers of apprenticeship programmes throughout the UK. Our numbers also increased dramatically when, in 2013, we merged with the training arm of The Pearson Group. The deal happened after I was called by the Group's CEO one weekend. The American company could not make a success of its mainly IT training arm, and it wanted us to turn it around at no cost to the college. As a result, we inherited several new campuses, some of which we eventually had to close, but overall, the deal boosted our reach considerably.

Being a champion of apprenticeship training put me in a good position to help shape national policy, and in 2017, I was appointed to be on the board of the Institute of Apprenticeships (IFA). While the organisation had been formed back in 2015 to oversee the design and delivery of apprenticeships, it only became operational two years later in 2017. The apprenticeship levy was also introduced at the same time.

The levy had been a long time in the making. First announced by David Cameron's government back in 2015, it asked employers with an annual pay bill of more than £3m to pay a sum to government to fund apprenticeship programmes. However, it was not without resistance, and I remember watching the Prime Minister being put under the spotlight with some very difficult questions from industry at an event held by the Confederation of British Industries (CBI). Nevertheless, I supported the thrust of the levy. Other countries such as Germany and Switzerland had developed very successful apprenticeship programmes, and I felt that without a proper partnership between government, education and employers, the UK was in danger of being left behind. Also, some of the UK's most successful industrialists had taken the apprenticeship route, yet somehow it had lost its prestige, even though for many it made practical sense. Apprentices earn up to 21% more than graduates after qualification. I saw how it could lift so many young people who were unsuited to an academic route or unable to pay university tuition fees out of a generational cycle of worklessness.

Moreover, I saw that a further education college like mine was pivotal in its delivery. However, while provision had been made for university and industry representation on the IFA board, no seat had been specifically earmarked for further education. I sought to change this, and when I landed this Cabinet Office position, I saw another opportunity to influence change. As it turned out, my voice was much needed. Delivery of the programme left a lot to be desired. We could see from early on that the system's complexity and bureaucratic red tape became a real barrier to engaging with it. A number of employers simply were not convinced by the scheme at all and decided it was easier just to pay the levy without any intention of offering the training. This left a pot of money sitting in Treasury coffers not helping the people it was designed to.

In effect, a policy that had been designed to increase apprenticeship numbers and raise productivity levels had the opposite effect, and we started to see a drop in our own numbers. While I was able to argue the point forcefully, it became very frustrating that this giant step forward by government was being hampered by poor delivery. By the time I stood down from the board towards the end of 2018, it was unclear just how successful the apprenticeship levy had been, and this remains so. In my opinion, there was a clear mismatch between the political vision behind this policy and its implementation in practice.

With a graduating student at our graduation ceremony at Kelham Hall, Nottinghamshire

Our annual graduation ceremony held at Kelham Hall, Nottinghamshire

A surprise visit of the leader of the Labour party, the Right Honourable Jeremy Corbyn to my college in 2017

8
Giving Back

'The best way not to feel hopeless is to get up and do something. Don't wait for good things to happen to you. If you go out and make some good things happen, you will fill the world with hope, you will fill yourself with hope'

Barack Obama

'Mansfield is the best place in the world'. This is the message I gave to my students and the message I sent out to the wider community. It was once a great place of productivity. Not so long ago, tens of thousands of men worked in the coal mines of West Nottinghamshire. Women there still have memories of operating the machines in the hosiery and knitwear mills. It was my firm belief that Mansfield could be great again.

I was also never in any doubt about the challenges that the area faced. Often, during my time there, I jumped into my car and drove around. I saw the estates and the boarded-up shops and the impact of factory closures. I saw a place struggling to flourish – beset by high unemployment and deprivation. However, one event really sticks in my mind. Not long after I had started at the college, one girl came to see me. She had just started work in the clothing department of a national supermarket chain.

'I want to thank you, Mrs Khemka,' she told me.

'Why?' I asked curiously.

'I have a job, and it's because you inspired me. My mother told me I would only amount to a prostitute'.

My heart hit the floor. I could not believe what I was hearing, and that evening, I arrived home in tears.

‘What is it, Asha?’ Shankar asked me.

The low expectation that had been placed on this girl both moved me and troubled me. As I explained to Shankar what had happened, a plan began to formulate. While the college catered for certain groups of students who could be encouraged and nurtured, those who were not in education, employment or training – the NEETS – were perilously close to being left behind altogether.

‘What can I do?’ I asked Shankar. I could not stand by and do nothing. Over the next few days, I had an idea to start my own charity, which I eventually called the Inspire and Achieve Foundation.

The charity itself took a bit of setting up, but by then I felt on a much surer footing about it making a difference. By 2008, I was much more knowledgeable about the area, and I understood some of its more difficult challenges. For example, teenage pregnancy was high, as was worklessness, combined with a high crime rate. The figures were startling. Youngsters not in education or training were costing the taxpayer £3.6bn in benefits. In Mansfield, the number of 17- to 19-year-olds claiming Jobseeker’s Allowance was 43% higher than the national average. To compound this, not long after my charity was born, the government announced it was to remove a £30-a-week education maintenance allowance that helped children overcome barriers to education and employment such as travel costs.

I wanted my charity to capture people who were the hardest to reach in society and engage them in a meaningful route through education. The problem was, I had never been involved in a charity before, let alone launched one. To start anything, you need money, and so, I began as I always have done: by educating myself and then finding a way. I rang people who I knew had some wealth but also who I felt would be sympathetic to my cause and asked them to back my project. For example, Professor Nathu Puri pledged his support from early on and agreed to be the chair. I am forever grateful for his enthusiasm, help and his initial pledge of £5,000 to support the charity. Likewise, Professor David Greenaway, Vice-Chancellor at the University of Nottingham, became an early patron, alongside the then-MP for Ashfield Gloria de Piero, and Paddy Tipping, the former MP for Sherwood.

I also spoke to people who I knew could help me develop a concrete plan, such as the CEO of the AoC, Martin Doel. From the outset, I was also delighted that my son Sneh was keen to sit on the board as a trustee.

His support came in an advisory capacity, as he was living in London and working for Bupa. I also began enrolling a team around me who were living locally and who also fully understood the conditions on the ground.

The overarching idea for Inspire and Achieve was to develop the area's hard-to-reach youth via a three-step plan. First of all, we had to find people. On the surface, it sounded easy, but in fact, engaging with hard-to-reach youth can be very challenging. Homelessness, for example, was not largely visible in the area but hidden. For this reason, we developed a peer-to-peer model and employed people who had been in the same situation themselves. This way, they knew the hubs that young people frequented. These included hostels, streets, shopping centres and markets – all the capture points where we could start to engage.

At first, I earmarked one of the college buildings to house the charity and sought some government funding because there was a skills and educational element to the journey. The centre was well equipped to provide appropriate skills training, including a workshop for repairing motorbikes. Although the charity's location has moved since, our aim to create a safe, secure environment with a culture of acceptance and understanding for children has remained. We also employ staff who are passionate, understand the challenges and have a will to engage with these young people.

The launch of Inspire and Achieve was very memorable, which took place in the House of Commons. Sneh and Shalini both joined me, alongside many notable people including the then-Defence Secretary Geoff Hoon MP and Sir Alan Meale MP. Nat Puri also lent his support. I shared my vision and delivered my speech with passion, so much so that Shalini told me afterwards that by the time I had finished, everybody wanted to donate.

'Mummy, you had the audience eating out of your palm,' she joked.

Geoff Hoon also commented about me, 'If Asha asks me to do something, I can't say no. I don't have an option!' This spurred me on and made me feel that I was succeeding.

Back in Mansfield, we started out by offering breakfast to people who engaged with the service. It was not much – just tea and toast or some fruit – but for many youngsters, it might have been their only meal of the day. The next step was to give these young people some affection and nurturing. This happened during a 12-week programme of activities ranging from a street art project, to boxing or fitness training, to cycling or a football club, and then moving them onto a skills and education pathway. Here, there was an element of classroom-based learning, which included courses in employability skills, anger management, confidence and presentation skills.

As well as activities and classes, we also paired young people with business mentors and encouraged them to take part in shadowing work programmes. Our aim is always to move a person to the next destination after being with us for 12 months. Whether this is an educational course, a job or helping them with a business idea of their own, each individual has their own starting point and their own unique journey to take.

Capturing and engaging people is only one part of the jigsaw. Retaining them is also a challenge. Many have safeguarding issues at home or responsibilities such as caring for siblings or a parent. For this reason, we want to track their journey, and if, at any point, they drop from the radar, our team will find them and attempt to re-engage with them.

In this past pandemic year, recidivism has been an even greater challenge for Inspire and Achieve. Social distancing has restricted access to young people's homes and the public areas where they might otherwise be found. For young people where safeguarding issues at home are a problem, the pandemic has also placed them at greater risk. There is only so much we can do via social media channels and Zoom. However, we have tried our best to overcome the challenges and move forwards.

Overall, our progression rates have been high, although it is always disappointing to lose any child in the system. By 2010, two years after the charity started, we had moved around 250 children into education or work. Since then, we have helped many, many more.

From the outset, I have been very fortunate to have a team of hard-working, dedicated staff who have always gone above and beyond their roles despite the challenging nature of the work. Aside from the incredible hard work that has gone into the charity over the past 13 years, we have also had a tremendous amount of fun. While my full-time role at the college meant I could not be overly involved in the charity's day-to-day affairs, I came into my own during our fundraising events both at the college and in London. On two occasions, I even donned a chef's hat and whites and cooked with chefs from the Mem-Saab Indian restaurant in Leicester at the college's fine-dining restaurant, Number 19 Brasserie.

Being a keen amateur cook myself and having been brought up on the best Indian cuisine, I was keen to enliven people's senses and tastebuds and introduce them to an authentic taste of home. Aubergine bhajis, lamb rogan josh, matar paneer and a whole host of other dishes were served to guests, including Geoff Hoon MP, who paid £10 for the lunch. In the end, 'The Principal Cooks' event, as we called it, raised a good sum of money.

As many of our friends were avid cricket fans, I decided to host fundraising gala dinners at Lord's Cricket Ground. Special guests included the former England cricket captain Graham Gooch and another former captain, Mike Gatting. The atmosphere in the famous Long Room was always electric, and Shankar and I recall many special moments. One of our favourite people was the veteran cricket player Farokh Engineer, who had played internationally for India and for Lancashire County Cricket Club in the UK. He is also a great friend of Nat Puri, who helped us invite him along. As it turned out, the flamboyant batsman and wicketkeeper was also a very funny MC, and he kept the crowd entertained all night. In particular, a joke he told about the Indian cricketer Sachin Tendulkar had our guests in stitches.

Apparently, the legendary batsman had gone to open a new bank account, but the bank clerk had not recognised him.

'Do you earn £100,000? You must do to qualify to be a member of this bank,' she told him.

Tendulkar paused before delivering his punchline, 'Some days I do. Some days I don't,' he shrugged.

As ever, Nat Puri used his own unique humour to charm guests into parting with their cash. Personally, I felt so uncomfortable asking people for money, but Nat did it with a smile on his face and a glint in his eye.

One time, I overheard him talking to the late Lord Noon. Gulam Noon was worth a staggering £75m, having made his money when he emigrated from Mumbai to the UK in the early 1970s. Here, from humble beginnings, he moved from owning a sweet shop in Southall to being a king of Indian foods.

'One day, you will die and lose all your wealth,' Nat said to him bluntly. 'While you are alive, why don't you put some of it to use? I am chairing the Inspire and Achieve Foundation, and it needs your help'. After that introduction, Lord Noon had no choice but to put his hand in his pocket.

The events in London were not just about raising money via auctions and telephone calls. I also made sure I took youngsters who had shown signs of confidence-building to come onto the stage with me to say a few words. For them, it was such a big occasion, but I wanted to build their self-esteem by giving them that exposure. In particular, I remember one girl who came to see me in the college.

'Mrs Khemka, you look so glamorous. I want to come with you when you go to London,' she pleaded with me. When the next event rolled around, I kept my promise and brought her along. I could see that she felt so special dressing up for the occasion and accompanying me. In a sense, it was overwhelming for her. She grew in confidence, and I knew that being part of something so memorable would inspire her to go on to achieve further. Later, she became a fashion designer herself.

Whenever I held an event, I always wore my best saris and my bindi. You could say it became my trademark. As the founder of the charity, I also found myself at Buckingham Palace for a second time after my OBE. For this, I picked out one of my most beautiful saris designed by Manish Malhotra, the fashion designer turned Bollywood stylist. At the reception at the palace, my outfit certainly caught the eye of Princess Michael of Kent, a very glamorous woman in her own right.

'You look so beautiful. I love your sari!' she told me.

Meanwhile, the Duke of Edinburgh was busy joking with the guests. To one Indian man, I overheard him say, 'Why did you run away from your country?' The man's answer, with a nod to India's occupation by the British Raj, had everybody laughing. 'Sir, because you brought the wealth here, and I followed,' he smiled.

More recently, the Inspire and Achieve Foundation has extended this royal connection working in partnership with Prince Charles's charity, The Prince's Trust, to help unemployed people between the ages of 16 and 26 gain new skills, increase their confidence and gain nationally recognised qualifications.

I am happy to say that more than a decade after I started the Inspire and Achieve Foundation, it is still going strong and still making a difference. The charity now employs around 35 people and stands on its own two feet. Perhaps I am little disappointed that I could never grow it into a national charity. The truth is, there was only so much I could juggle, and it would have been too much of an undertaking. That the charity continues to provide dedicated support to the local area – and does it well – still makes me incredibly proud.

It's Time To Give Back!

Asha's next ambition is to formally establish and lunch the Inspire and Achieve Foundation which will help make real the dreams of the young white working class.

At a dinner at The House of Commons recently, Asha launched the concept of the foundation amongst MPs, key business leaders and other significant VIPs.

Together with the help and knowledge from a number of business links and already successful relationship belonging to the College, this foundation aims to help disadvantaged young people to achieve their dreams in the future.

BIG HITTERS FORMER ENGLAND CAPTAIN JOINS RANGEMORE WOMAN'S MISSION TO INSPIRE YOUNG PEOPLE TO ACHIEVE THEIR FULL POTENTIAL

A CHARITABLE foundation set up by a Rangemore woman is celebrating a major cash boost.

The Inspire and Achieve Foundation, created by Asha Khemka, raised more than £33,000 by staging its second annual gala fund-raising dinner at Lord's Cricket Ground.

More than 100 guests from business, commerce and education attended the black-tie dinner and charity auction in the historic Long Room at the 'home of cricket'.

Ex-England hockey player Roger Dakin introduced the evening's proceedings and the guest speaker was former England cricket captain Mike Gatting.

Mrs Khemka, principal and chief executive of West Nottinghamshire College, said: "The event was a fantastic success, both in terms of boosting funds and shining the spotlight on the very serious issue of youth unemployment.

"It was heartening to bring together people who share a passion for raising the aspirations and achievements of young people in our society.

"I'm immensely grateful to everybody that attended and am truly humbled by the amount raised."

Mrs Khemka, who is married to Shankar Khemka, senior consultant orthopaedic surgeon at Burton's Queen's Hospital, launched the foundation in 2008 after growing increasingly concerned about the rise in young people not in education, employment or training.

INSPIRATIONS... former England cricket captain Mike Gatting and Asha Khemka.

Burton Mail

Friday, July 15, 2011

With Mike Gatting OBE, former England cricket captain at Lord's cricket ground during an Inspire & Achieve fundraising gala dinner

From a small town in India to being handed a Damehood, the life of Asha Khemka has been remarkable. The Rangemore resident spent half of her life raising three children before heading into education, eventually being recognised by the Queen. ROB SMYTH uncovers a fascinating and inspirational tale.

Bowled over!

WEST Notts College principal Asha Khemka is joined by former England cricket captain Graham Gooch at a fundraising gala dinner at Lord's Cricket Ground to raise money for a charity she set up.

The black-tie dinner and auction event - which included speeches by Mr Gooch and former Indian cricketer and current IPL referee Farokh Engineer and around 100 guests - raised more than £40,000 for Mrs Khemka's Inspire and Achieve Foundation to create a centre in Mansfield for young people not in education, employment or training, known as NEETs.

With Graham Gooch, former England cricket captain at Lord's cricket ground during an Inspire & Achieve fundraising gala dinner

9

Bridging Continents

'Travelling is an essential part of everyone's personal growth... Books are where education starts. Experience is where it continues. The power of those real memories is stronger than just reading facts. It shapes who we become and stays with us forever'

Colin Edward Slais

At the start of every term, I always spoke to staff about what adventures I had had during the holidays. Part of me wanted to relive my holidays, as the memory always fades, but it was mainly a way of telling people that we had recharged my batteries. Now that term time was upon us, it was time for the hard work to begin. That said, as Shankar and I became more established in our careers, we wanted to travel more – a luxury we never had when we were in India or in the early days of bringing up our children. So, during our breaks, we made a point of discovering new and exciting corners of the world.

Some highlights come to our minds. One Easter break, we travelled by car with Shalini from Seattle along the Rocky Mountain route through the stunning scenery of Jasper and Banff. Walking on the frozen lake in Banff and watching the emerald-green beauty of Jasper Lake was an awe-inspiring experience I can never forget.

Later, Shankar and I went back and took a train journey through the Rocky Mountains, its glass roof allowing us to take in the glistening lakes, thundering waterfalls and rugged snow-capped mountain tops. When, on the same trip, we took an Alaskan cruise, I could not believe my eyes. I was lost in my own world running on the treadmill in the gym when I looked up to see the most dramatic glacier towering over me, sparkling black and blue in the sunlight. When I made my way out onto the balcony to take it in, I watched as dolphins raced alongside the ship. During the same trip, we took a whale-watching excursion, and when our small ship reached the spot where whales could be seen in the distance, a microphone was lowered into the water. Suddenly, we could hear an orchestra of whales singing beautifully. As the boat sailed even closer, they treated us to a theatrical show of synchronised swimming. At this, a childlike excitement spread over me as I watched them leap in and out of the water in sequence.

On another holiday in Cape Town, South Africa, we watched in awe as the sun rose across the bay, reflecting Table Mountain serenely in the water. On Robben Island, we fell silent at the pain of the Apartheid era as we stared at the bullet holes pockmarking the prison cell walls, before walking across the sand and stones that Nelson Mandela and his fellow prisoners were forced to dig during their many years of imprisonment there.

In Australia, we visited the sacred mountain of Uluru. We were lucky enough to enjoy the panorama of the rock during sunrise and sunset. During our trip to the Great Barrier Reef, we could not believe our eyes when we saw the vast underwater world with countless varieties of colourful fish, the never-ending coral reefs and gigantic tortoises swimming so gracefully.

In New Zealand, we breathed in the smoke and sulphur of the hot springs and geysers and watched as the lakes changed from green to yellow to red. We also visited Christchurch, a beautiful city with spiritual surroundings but sadly ravaged by a massive earthquake which, heartbreakingly, had left its buildings devastated. Landing by helicopter on Mount Cook among the glaciers and seeing aqua-blue lakes in the distance was as mesmerising as flying over Mount Everest on a trip to Nepal a few years before. Then, we had caught the clearest of days and flown so close that it felt like we could almost touch its peak.

In Cambodia, our children had kindly treated us to an exquisite evening to celebrate our wedding anniversary: a horse-drawn carriage took us from our hotel to a small farmhouse with open corn fields, where a red carpet was laid out for us. There, we watched as chefs created a seven-course vegetarian meal. How can we ever forget the music serenading us, the hundreds of candles that burned brightly in the field and the stars that shone above us?

In many ways, our travels were a reminder of how our world had become far more expansive compared to the life we had left behind. There was – and still is – so much more to discover.

While Shankar and I travelled more for pleasure, I also began travelling more for work. As I continued to be recognised nationally, more chances to broaden horizons abroad came my way. As ever, I grabbed the opportunities.

In particular, my work on the board of the AoC opened up a new international landscape for me. There, I had met lots of people who shared my energy and passion for education. In particular, I came into contact with Matthew Hancock MP, who was the then-Minister for Skills. I had met him as part of the many roundtable discussions I was taking part in on policy. One of the first times I met him was at a meeting in his office in Whitehall. Immediately, I noticed that the sweater he was wearing had holes in it, and admittedly, I felt a little motherly towards him.

'Why are you wearing this?' I asked. Being a perfectionist when it came to style, I found it hard to understand.

'It's the moths,' he replied, unconcerned that the sweater looked terrible.

Not long after, when I attended a speech that he was making at the Cabinet Office, I noticed he had the same moth-eaten sweater on. I could barely watch. Instead of listening to his speech, I slipped out and bought him a new jumper, slipped back into the room and marched on stage.

'Matthew, take your sweater off,' I ordered him.

'I can't say no to this!' he laughed as he wrestled his pullover over his neck, the audience speechless at what was unfolding on stage. It is a story Matthew and I would recall time and time again.

Soon, we had the opportunity to travel together to Delhi. Matthew was heavily involved in the AoC, and there was an idea to expand the network in a country where the development of vocational skills was increasingly becoming vital. Far from being the underdeveloped nation India was when Shankar and I left, its industrial economy was booming. By 2013, many countries were eyeing it as a destination to build university campuses and widen their reach. An estimated 500 million young people in India would require vocational training over the next decade, and there was a danger Britain could miss out.

'Asha, could you lead on this project?' the board asked me. In truth, I was anxious about saying yes. India is still a very patriarchal society, and I felt that an Indian woman heading the delegation and the project may be detrimental to its success. It felt like a defeat saying it, but perhaps a white male might be better received? The board, however, were having none of it and persuaded me to act as chair. 'No, Asha. It has to be you,' people insisted.

As it turned out, the whole trip was to be a very emotional journey for me. Forging educational links between the two countries had been a dream of mine for some time, but gathering together more than 30 colleges from the UK to meet India's growing demand for skills felt exhilarating. In particular, I wanted English students to witness the energy and drive of their Indian counterparts. At the same time, Indian students could understand what proper, professional vocational training looked and felt like.

Matthew kindly agreed to host the launch of the initiative within the luxurious setting of the British High Commission in Delhi that January in front of a VIP delegation. Around 100 Indian and UK skills providers, industrial partners, government ministers and civil servants all came together to hear a succession of speakers. When it came to my turn to deliver my speech, I talked for 45 minutes. I spoke about how transformational the project could be, but all the time I was speaking, it struck me how much I had transformed.

In the front row, my family had come from Sitamarhi to hear me. Shankar was also there beside my uncle, Ram Sharan, for whom I had so much respect. For the first time, they saw me not as the girl who had left Bihar but as a woman successful in her own right, making an impact on the world stage. As I looked down, Shankar's eyes had filled with tears, and I saw only love and admiration in the faces of my relatives. Such a unique moment for me was made all the more special by their presence. And when Ram Sharan Chacha approached one lady, Susan Pember CBE, who was also a trailblazer in the UK education sector afterwards, he, too, became very emotional.

'Thank you to England for giving Asha this opportunity,' he said to her, amazed at how the country had allowed me to prosper.

'No. We should be thanking you for providing us with the queen of our education system,' she replied. I was very touched when I heard this remark.

That week was spent travelling from city to city and connecting our delegates to the many educational establishments and businesses across the continent. It was a great start, but in the end, AoC India became harder to progress. While I could successfully connect people, the initiative required member colleges to develop the setup and training programme themselves. However, with budget cuts continually affecting FE colleges in the UK, India became less of a priority. Nevertheless, I felt we achieved something over the time that AoC India was operational that meant more than just talk.

That same year, I set foot back in India, and this time was to be another moment in Khemka family history. David Cameron, the then-prime minister of Britain's coalition government, was leading a delegation to strengthen ties between UK and Indian business, education and commerce. Similar delegations had gone before, but again, there had been no representation from the FE sector. Prior to this trip, I remember turning to my good friend John Cridland, then the Director-General of the CBI, to ask whether FE might get a seat at the table.

'I will move heaven and earth for you, Asha, but it will be difficult,' he said. John had visited the college and had been a very loyal supporter of my work there, but he also understood the poor recognition FE had had historically within government. He, too, wanted this to change, and in 2013, he advocated my becoming one of the first people from the FE sector to embark on such a delegation.

It was not the first time I had met David Cameron. Back in 2010, Shankar and I had been invited to the Diwali celebrations at 10 Downing Street, where we had been briefly introduced. Filling the room were many Indians who had made a contribution to British society, including Lord Karan Bilimoria CBE, DL, Baroness Verma and Lord Popat. I recall how poignant it was to watch the Prime Minister light the Diwali light at a colourful ceremony. As for David Cameron himself, I found him a dashing man, but even I could not have predicted how I would get to know him better during our trip to India.

Perhaps Shankar had had a premonition, but before I left for the airport, he handed me a few brochures advertising the college. 'Try and give these to David Cameron,' he told me. I had almost forgotten about them by the time the Prime Minister welcomed us in the executive lounge before boarding. On the flight, I was seated next to the Vice-Chancellor of Cambridge University and a woman who seemed to know the crew well (hence the champagne was flowing). Maybe that gave me a little Dutch courage, but I remembered the booklets and made it my mission to talk to David Cameron, even though he was seated in business class with the lords and baronesses.

‘I’d like to see the Prime Minister,’ I said as his private secretary appeared.

‘Mam, that’s probably not possible,’ he replied very politely, but just as I did not take no for an answer at the reception desk at Oswestry College all those years ago, I did not take no for an answer then.

‘You can do it,’ I smiled at him, and within a few minutes, I was in front of David Cameron, handing a booklet to him and asking if he would come to the college to visit. As I was led back to my seat, I felt pleased at what I had accomplished, but I had no idea of the impression it made. That night, still dressed in my suit, I laid a blanket out between the aisles and caught a wink of sleep before we began our descent into Mumbai. At the crack of dawn, just as I was adjusting my clothes and tidying my hair, a woman rushed up to me.

‘You’re Mrs Khemka, aren’t you?’ she said, before explaining that the Prime Minister had asked me to accompany him down the steps of the plane.

‘Do I have time to put my sari on?’ I pleaded with her. I was landing in my homeland, and I wanted to look smart, after all.

‘I’m so sorry. There’s no time. The plane is about to land,’ she replied hurriedly. I barely had a moment to grab my briefcase before I was led to the front of the plane past other government figures such as Priti Patel MP and Lord Popat to where David Cameron was waiting.

‘It was really nice to meet you. I’ve had a look at your college brochure, and it’s very impressive,’ he said, before gesturing that we disembark. As I made my way down the stairs, I almost had to pinch myself. As the hot wind hit my face, all I could hear was the clicking of cameras. And when I finally spoke to Shankar that evening, he could barely believe it either. His jaw had hit the floor when he had switched on the BBC One O’clock News back in Britain to see his wife coming down the steps beside the Prime Minister.

‘How did you do it?’ he asked me. The truth was, I was not sure myself. What I did know was that David Cameron’s visit was all about making an impact, and I was happy to be part of it. It is the only time I have ever seen the streets of Mumbai cleared of cars and rickshaws. When we reached the famous Taj Mahal Hotel, the roads outside also had fallen silent. It was the strangest feeling.

That week, during one of the meetings in Delhi, led by then Education Secretary David Willetts MP, I had the privilege of signing a memorandum of understanding with Mr C Banerjee, the Director-General of The Confederation of Indian Industries (CII), in the presence of Dr P Purandeswary, Indian Minister for Industry and Commerce. Then, after several more meetings in a variety of cities, it was time to return, but this was also not without its drama. During the trip, David Cameron had travelled to Amritsar, where he paid tribute to the victims of the 1919 Jallianwala Bagh massacre. At that time, led by General Dyer, the British had opened fire on hundreds of peaceful pro-independence protestors. No serving British prime minister had ever acknowledged this shameful event, let alone visited the site, but the press were already ripping into David Cameron for not issuing a formal apology. After the plane had taxied from the runway and we were airborne, he made a point of finding me.

While he was sitting beside me briefly, we had a conversation about his visit to Amritsar, and he seemed troubled by the comments made in the Indian media. Thankfully, I was able to provide a more balanced view. My uncle Ram Sharan, who was also unhappy with the comments made in the press, had emailed me and expressed his gratitude that David Cameron had visited Amritsar. Fortunately, I was able to show him what he had written. The letter was addressed to His Excellency Mr Prime Minister. It read:

> *Most humbly and respectfully, I wish to express that today your visit to Jallianwala Bagh is going to be a new page in the history of the Indo-British relationship. My eyes are full of tears. I salute you. This visit has become a vision for millions to look beyond the past. What has happened today is the value both nations believe in. Long live wisdom! I pray for your kind permission to address you as Dear David Cameron, without compromising the dignity of your office. Now, Dyer is history. Dear David-Cameron is present-future. Long live dear David Cameron!*

On reading it, I noticed that the Prime Minister seemed touched and appreciative of the gesture.

A year on from our trip together, I was honoured to be presented with the Woman of the Year Award at a glittering ceremony held in London. The award, handed to me by David Cameron, represented everything I had worked so hard to achieve in this country and also reflected the contribution that all ethnic minorities, not just myself, can make in building a better society. I can barely put into words the sense of joy I had in my heart when my name was called and the Prime Minister offered me his hand to step onto the stage. I was even more pleased when he addressed me as his friend and recalled our trip to India together and how delighted he was to present this award to me. In his speech, he said, 'In Britain today, there are still too few people from ethnic minorities in top positions,' adding that one day, he wanted to hear the title of prime minister followed by a British Asian name.

In my address, I wanted to encapsulate the two different worlds that had gifted the opportunities for success to me: 'I am truly humbled by this award. I often say: India made me, and Britain enabled me. My heart lies in India and my soul in Britain,' I told the crowd.

Of course, my success also meant I was constantly in a position to challenge power. While I was always very pleased to be selected to accompany government ministers on similar Indo-British trade delegations, I was concerned by the lack of follow-up. There was a lot of fanfare, but I worried that too many important people played lip service to deepening ties between the two countries. On the ground, not enough progress was being made. There were several times when I openly expressed my frustration and also repeated the frustration that Indian students had about coming to the UK. On the one hand, government rhetoric welcomed them in to learn, but on the other hand, these students were finding it impossible to get visas. I remember a few years later challenging Boris Johnson's brother, Jo, who was an education minister, on exactly the same matter when I accompanied him to India. There, students in Mumbai had grilled him, telling him, 'We want to learn from you, but you are not giving us visas!' If we had any hope of making our mark in India, the system had to change, I impressed upon him.

On another occasion, not long after my memorable trip with David Cameron, I accompanied the deputy prime minister, Liberal Democrat MP Nick Clegg, to Mumbai as a member of his delegation. At a reception at the Taj Hotel, Nick Clegg announced an inaugural award to honour Dadabhai Naoroji – a man who originated from Mumbai and was the first Indian MP in the UK Parliament in 1892. He also brought the first Indian businesses to Britain. The award was destined for someone who had made a significant contribution in developing partnerships between the two countries.

Not long after I returned, in January 2015, I was invited to join Nick Clegg for afternoon tea, and I was pleasantly surprised when he told me that I had been chosen as the person to receive this award. That same evening at the main reception of the Commonwealth Summit in London, the award was presented to me jointly by Nick Clegg and Sushma Swaraj, the Indian Foreign Minister. Later, I learned it had been Martin Doel at the AoC who had nominated me for my contribution in the field of education.

Subsequent trips to India were alongside Greg Clark MP, Minister for Universities and Science, who asked me to be part of a delegation at the UK–India Science and Innovation Council, and also Sajid Javid MP, who was the then-Secretary of State for Business, Innovation and Skills. At the time, I had been working with him on a project to drive up skills and to increase productivity in the Midlands called the Midlands Engine.

With the work of AoC India in full swing, new partnerships were also being created between some of the UK colleges and the Indian education system. As Chair of AoC India, I was invited to be a keynote speaker at a higher education event organised by the Federation of Indian Chambers of Commerce and Industry (FICCI) in Delhi. The event was opened by Smriti Irani, the Union Minister for Human Resource Development, who spoke about India's long and venerable education history. The country was known to have been home to the world's first university, established in Taxila in 700 BC. The spotlight now is on regenerating higher education in earnest to capitalise on India's burgeoning young population.

This time, I was accompanied by my good friends Dawn Ward, Principal of Burton and South Derbyshire College, and Stella Mbubaegbu, then Principal of Highbury College in Portsmouth. Delhi, it seemed, was always at the epicentre of excitement. Not long after we arrived and three days before my keynote speech, I was stepping out of the bath when suddenly and unexpectedly, I slipped on the marble floor. I remember very little about falling, but I must have been out cold for a few seconds. With my pulse still racing, I came to and hauled myself up to sit down, but moments later, a wave of dizziness washed over me.

'I've fallen. Could you please send someone?' I said faintly when I rang the reception, thinking that I should get some medical assistance. Within moments, hotel staff and managers were crowding around my door.

'Mrs Khemka, are you OK?' they knocked worriedly. I was their guest, and naturally, they were concerned. To my eternal gratitude, Stella and Dawn also dropped everything and rushed to be by my side.

Not long after, when I was eventually taken to hospital, staff rang my uncle Ram Sharan in Sitamarhi, who also travelled to be with me. I was very glad to see him. As it turned out, I had suffered a hairline fracture of the skull, but I did not let my injury prevent me from delivering my speech!

China and Malaysia were also destinations where I witnessed first-hand the sheer passion of the students, and I visited twice as a guest of Nottingham University, the council of which I served on for eight years. There, the university had established campuses in the city of Ningbo, a major industrial hub 140 miles south of Shanghai, and in Kuala Lumpur. The experience of meeting students, who were gathered from 70 different countries all around the world under one roof, was unique for me. The fact that board and lodging were cheaper compared to the UK made it affordable for students to gain qualifications from a world-class university like Nottingham.

Shankar accompanied me on the second trip, and we were taken aback by how many students had progressed through the ranks, graduated and were already making an impact in their home countries. What was also particularly touching was that the students who were guiding us had compiled and presented us with a photo album of memories, which we will cherish forever.

Another memorable visit was in January 2015 to the Cordia Institute in Sanghol in the western Punjab region. The institute, set up by Lord Diljit Rana, was established to transform the lives of rural youth through world-class educational opportunities, in particular in business management and the hospitality sector, where Lord Rana has focussed many of his own business interests back in Northern Ireland. I was invited to open the Construction Centre, which was built in partnership with West Nottinghamshire College. During this visit, I was surprised and honoured to see my face emblazoned on billboards around the institute. Following my speech, I had the pleasure of meeting with students. As I made my way along the line of youngsters welcoming me, I picked out one boy.

'What made you interested in study?' I asked him. He looked a little shy, and he hesitated slightly. As he did, one of Lord Rana's staff stepped in quickly.

'Asha, mam, this student won't be able to give you the answers,' he said. Momentarily, I thought about his comment, and I could feel a quiet rage rise up inside of me.

'Please do let me speak to him,' I told him. After, I stayed with the student and made a point of talking to him and bringing him out of his shell. Just as I thought, he was very capable of answering all my questions; he just needed the right encouragement. What I did not realise was that Lord Rana was only metres behind and had seen the story unfold for himself.

'I can see why you are where you are, Asha,' he told me. 'You are giving people importance, respecting them as individuals and letting them grow'. He did not know it, but Lord Rana's comment embodied everything I set out to do at West Nottinghamshire College.

Following a visit to my college by some of the members of the Australian Technical and Further Education (TAFE) institutes, I was also invited to Australia as a keynote speaker to their annual congress in Adelaide in 2016. I found this to be one of the most educational and illuminating experiences I had ever had. My speech covered the topic 'Regenerating Communities through Leadership,' and I was able to take my audience through my own journey of leadership and the work I had done in raising the aspirations of our youth back home. I felt humbled to receive warm and affectionate compliments from delegates, and on the previous evening, when the mayor of Adelaide had hosted a reception at the Oval Cricket Ground, I felt similarly honoured by the kind words he spoke about me in his introduction.

What I was most struck by was how Australia had been very proactive in recognising its own skills shortage and had taken steps to allow more immigration to plug the gap. Although my hosts there looked up to Britain as an exemplar of vocational training, I told them how advanced their thinking was. Moreover, Australia does not seem to be beset culturally by some of the snobbery that exists in Britain associated with FE, and that sadly still exists today.

'You are doing an amazing job,' I reassured them.

Government officials in the cities of Brisbane, Melbourne, Adelaide and Canberra also met with me. They were keen to learn how the UK was preparing to bring in its planned apprenticeship levy, and I gave presentations on it and other policy changes that were in the pipeline by then.

In 2017, I received an invitation to participate and speak at the Festival of Education, taking place in the city of Jaipur in Rajasthan. I was particularly delighted because Rajasthan is our ancestral place. Receiving a warm welcome from the chief minister, Mrs Vasundhara Raje, at my presence there was immensely humbling for me. My first visit to Jaipur was in 2007 when I had met her with my proposal of education partnership. This time, almost a decade later, I returned as her guest to speak.

My most recent educational visit was in December 2018 when I was privileged enough to visit the Kalinga Institute of Social Sciences in Bhubaneshwar in the eastern Indian state of Orissa. Founded in 1992, the institute was set up by an Indian educationalist, philanthropist and true visionary, Achyuta Samanta, a tireless campaigner for empowerment through education. Dr Samanta himself grew up in abject poverty after his father died when he was four, leaving behind his widowed mother and eight children. In almost three decades, he has grown the institute to cater for 25,000 children, all from tribal backgrounds in India. Ordinarily, these children would not receive any education at all, but the institute feeds, clothes, cares for and looks after them from the age of five right through to the completion of their university education at age 22.

The experience was altogether overwhelming. In the vast hall, I looked out onto schoolgirls and boys who were neatly lined up and cross-legged in their pink and blue salwar suits and school uniforms. Even though almost 10,000 students were sitting on the floor, at first, it was so quiet that I could have heard a pin drop. Then, I began. 'Believe in yourself, and don't let anyone tell you any different,' I impressed upon them. In fact, after my opening words, I could barely get through my speech. Every five minutes, the hall erupted with applause, and hands shot up with so many questions.

'Asha, mam, can you please tell us why you left this country?' It was a difficult question and one at their age I would never have been able to answer.

'I was not as lucky as you to have this support structure,' I said. Suddenly, my mind was cast back to my sadness at having to leave school to look after my mother and then again leaving school to be married at such a young age.

'So, mam, are you saying if we are forced to be married, we can still achieve?' another young girl asked me.

I looked at her and saw my own self reflected back at me. 'Yes, but make sure that you stand on your own two feet. Know who you are and exactly what it is that you want,' I replied.

I was overwhelmed by the reception and warmth given to both myself and Shankar. Our welcome there was extended beyond the campus of the institute. The next morning, we were driven to visit the historical Konark Temple and also Jagannath Temple in Puri, a most sacred pilgrimage for Hindus, made all the more special as this was something Shankar and I had both desired to do one day in our lives.

The famous and the most iconic monument ever built, the "Taj Mahal' takes your breath away and to be there together is an unforgettable memory

With my flying friends on a visit to Amsterdam

With my daughter Shalini, relaxing and enjoying the breathtaking views of the beautiful Emerald Lake in Jasper, Canada

Stepping down the plane on Mumbai airport with the British Prime Minister the Right Honourable David Cameron during his trade mission to India in 2013

Signing a MOU with the Director-General of CII (Confederation of Indian industry) Mr Chandrajit Banerjee in the presence of the Right Honourable David Willets, British education secretary and the Indian Minister for Industry and Commerce Dr P Purandeswary in New Delhi in 2013

The British Prime Minister the Right Honourable David Cameron presenting my 'Woman of the Year' award at the annual GG2 leadership awards ceremony in London in November 2014

The British Deputy Prime Minister the Right Honourable Nick Clegg along with Her Excellency Sushma Swaraj the Indian Foreign Minister and the Right Honourable Priti Patel MP presenting me with the inaugural 'Dadabhai Naoroji' award at the Commonwealth summit in London in October 2014

Opening the International skills summit in the presence of the governor of Kerala along with other dignitaries in Trivandrum in February 2016

Laying the foundation stone for the construction centre at the Cordia Institute of Higher Education in Sanghol, Punjab at the kind invitation of Lord Diljit Rana MBE in 2015

Delivering my keynote address at the Annual TAFE (technical and further education) Convention in Adelaide, invited by the TAFE directors Australia in September 2017

Invited as a keynote speaker by Her Excellency Vasundhara Raje, the Chief Minister of Rajasthan during the Skills Festival in Jaipur in August 2017

At a dinner at Rambagh Palace in Jaipur with Akshay Kumar, the most versatile actor of Hindi Cinema for the last three decades during the Skills Summit

Landing on top of Mount Cook, the highest mountain in New Zealand, a memorable experience during our holiday

Both Shankar and I were mesmerised admiring the beauty of the Himalayan mountain range from the top of the hill during our holiday in Mussoorie

Addressing and greeted by almost 10,000 boys and girls of tribal community of Odisha at the Kalinga Institute of Social Sciences in Bhubaneswar in December 2018

Returning to my old school almost after 54 years and greeted by the staff and students at Kamala Girls High School, Sitamarhi, in December 2018 and being presented with my old school records

10

To Live and to Learn

'A good leader takes a little more than his share of the blame and a little less than his share of the credit'

Arnold Glasow

In 2014, I was given the greatest honour of my life and of my career. I received a Damehood. For me, this was the culmination of many years of determination and hard work – not just for my own leadership role at West Nottinghamshire College but for everyone who had helped me make the college a success and create a strong impact both nationally and internationally.

By that year, not only had we raised standards, but we had also realised our dream of rebuilding. Alongside the Construction and Skills Centre that we opened in 2009, we also completed a £24m redevelopment project that included a centre for the creative industries, housing a 150-seat performance theatre, dance studios, live music rooms, editing suites and a TV studio. Our fine-dining restaurant had also opened its doors, and I spent many hours on its reception making sure its quality was maintained. Such was my attention to detail that I even rang in regularly, disguising my voice to book a table, just to see that the service being offered by students was impeccable.

Also unveiled was a professional health and beauty spa, a state-of-the-art hair and beauty salon, plus new classrooms. We were delighted when Toni Mascolo of Toni & Guy accepted our invitation to open these officially.

In 2012, a new sports hall also opened, boasting six courts for a variety of sports, and a science laboratory. That same year, we enjoyed another royal visit – this time from Prince Andrew, who toured our new campus. All in all, the college had come a long way from the first day I stepped into it to present my vision. Now, with its trademark tomato-red exterior, it was the bold, iconic gateway to Mansfield I had always imagined. Even its name had changed; we rebranded the college 'Vision West Nottinghamshire College'.

When I discovered I was to be made a Dame, it only impressed upon me how important that journey had been. Just like my OBE, the letter itself came via the Cabinet Office, and I was instructed to keep the news quiet until my name was announced in the New Year Honours List of 2014. As soon as that happened, I was overwhelmed at the response from people, especially those who had supported me. Matthew Hancock MP wrote to tell me it was an honour 'richly deserved'. The governors at the AoC recognised what a 'special and unusual honour this is in the FE sector'. The lord-lieutenants of both Nottinghamshire and Staffordshire sent me their 'warmest congratulations'. Lord Bilimoria called me 'tirelessly innovative' and 'one of the pioneers in the country,' and Baroness Thornton commented that, 'The award will give added esteem – if more were needed – to the tireless energy you have put into your work of empowering people through education'. For those kind words and many, many more, I am eternally grateful.

Perhaps the most touching messages came from family and friends. My eldest uncle, Devi Chacha, wrote to me from India reminding me that my award was based on merit, recognised regardless of cast or creed. My children also sent me a beautiful message: 'Before the world recognised you, we, your family, did. For being the best wife and mother, one could ever hope for'. The card was signed off with the words: 'We salute you, Mummy. Dame of our hearts!'

Later that year, I attended Buckingham Palace once again. On arrival at the palace, recipients of CBEs, Knighthoods and Damehoods were all escorted to a grand room ready for the investiture ceremony. Ladies in beautiful hats and gloves, and men – some in top hats and tails – all gathered in the first-floor room, and it was a pleasure to meet them all. Looking around, it was almost like a fairy-tale experience. Under the guild decorations and portraits of kings and queens, the butlers served refreshments. Outwardly, dressed in my gold sari and jewellery purchased during my last trip to India, I looked confident and proud, even though I was a little nervous inside.

When it came time to enter the hall ready for the awards ceremony, I was asked to lead the party, as I was the only recipient that day to be honoured with a Damehood. Suddenly, I felt as overwhelmed as I had done five decades before. It was as if I was a young bride again, stepping through the doors of Shankar's family home for the first time. Yet, this occasion was also completely different, I was not wearing a veil this time and I was leading and not following.

In the audience, I caught a glimpse of my family, and just as I was approaching the stage, I saw Shankar sitting proudly and smiling at me. Sheel and Sneh looked so handsome and could not take their eyes off me, and Shalini looked stunningly pretty. Her face was glowing with pride and happiness, and I saw tears rolling down her cheeks like pearls. Afterwards, she told me how overwhelmed she had felt when she reflected on my 40-year journey from Bihar to Buckingham Palace.

I was presented with the grand cross, this time by HRH Prince Charles. 'Lovely to see you again, Dame Asha,' he commented as he pinned it to my sari and shook my hand while I curtsied. By now, my curtsy was becoming quite polished! The story was covered widely by newspapers and television both here and in Asian countries. In particular, many highlighted the unique journey I had made through the education system. Although I was not aware of it until others told me, I am only the second woman of Indian origin to be awarded the top British honour since the order was instituted in 1917, the first being Maharani Lakshmi Devi of Dhar in 1931 during the British Raj. I also recall one person asking me, 'How do you have the confidence to wear a sari to the palace?' My reply was simple: 'It's not about confidence. It's who I am'.

Afterwards, the college arranged a celebration of achievement at the St James's Court Hotel. This was attended by friends and family, colleagues, many representatives from the FE sector and the various boards I sat on, plus many supporters – figures like John Cridland from the CBI, who said that when he heard I had been made a dame, he leapt with joy. During the evening, we treated guests to a Marwari feast – the many dishes of our ancestors from Rajasthan. My friend Matthew Hancock MP gave the keynote speech. Lord Karan Bilimoria CBE, DL, and others who had watched my journey, also said a few words. Shalini followed with a very personal speech, telling our family story from the moment we set foot in the UK that snowy January day in 1978, to setting up home in Oswestry, to becoming principal and CEO of West Nottinghamshire College. She said:

> *It seems only yesterday that she was a housewife struggling to support her family in a new country. To get from there has brought into sharp relief her true attributes both professionally and at home of perseverance, dedication, determination, involvement, communication, kindness, love and leadership. She has always delivered this with a passionate championing of the basic tenet of education being the route to success.*

In my thank-you speech, I paid tribute to all the people who helped me along the way. Alongside my family, I thanked Jean Hardy, my long-term mentor, and everyone else who made the journey possible. At its close, I remembered the words of Dr Abdul Kalam, who I had had the pleasure of meeting seven years before and who had asked me what my page would be in the book of life. I said:

> *My page will be the page of learning. Friends, I want to thank you for being co-authors on my page of learning. Tonight, I salute you for being part of my journey. I am indebted to Britain for giving me life-enhancing opportunities.*

Meanwhile, as I was in London celebrating my investiture, TV crews overran the college in Mansfield. The head of the students' union was interviewed for the lunchtime news and was asked her opinion on whether I should be made a Dame. Fortunately, she said yes, the reason being the many positive changes I had brought to the college. Many of the students were also asked what they thought of me. 'She's a superstar!' one student cried. To my delight, the closing shot was of a group of students gathered in the sports hall shouting, 'Hip hip hooray!' To be recognised by peers was one thing, but to be congratulated like that by students was quite something else. Their approval made everything we had achieved worthwhile.

Over the next few years, all the milestones we had set our minds to were achieved. The range of our new facilities was being enjoyed by a record number of students. In late 2014, Lord Bilimoria opened our new studio school, which started out by catering for 125 students aged between 14 and 19 who would specialise in either engineering and transport, or healthcare. In particular, he commented on the students' enthusiasm and commitment.

Never a person to rest on my laurels, by 2015, I looked again to the future. Having grown the curriculum to encompass a full range of qualifications from vocational training to A-levels, it had always been my dream that Mansfield would become a university town. That year, we took a step closer when a £6.5m project to build a university centre was given the green light. As well as offering students full honours degrees, it would also be a centre for advanced apprenticeships and those wanting to study part-time professional qualifications. For me, it was vital that we continued to equip young people and adults with higher-level skills and qualifications for an increasingly competitive jobs market.

As well as progress being made at the college and my own growing reputation outside, I was also becoming quite a regular at Buckingham Palace. Not long after my damehood, I was invited by Her Majesty the Queen to a private lunch. This time, it was a more intimate affair. There were no TV crews or family alongside me. Instead, I arrived to be seated in a room near to the dining hall with four other invited guests. Beforehand, I had thought very hard about what gift I would take to the Queen. After all, the Queen is a woman who has everything. Besides, I wanted the present to be meaningful and representative of the college and its students. With Mansfield being a former mining community, I eventually settled on the most beautiful brass miner's lamp in its own presentation case. I also brought with me a card made and signed by the students at the college.

'What an appropriate gift. Thank you for bringing it. Please take my gratitude back to the college,' Her Majesty said as she welcomed me in. Soon, we were led into the dining hall where we enjoyed a seven-course lunch, my courses all being vegetarian. Unexpectedly, I was seated next to the Queen, and the Duke of Edinburgh sat opposite us. I felt I had to tell her how much admiration I had for her poise and her grace. 'The way you present yourself, the way you stand and walk, the way you hold yourself, it's something to be admired,' I told her. The Queen's reply was short and sweet: 'One gets used to it,' she smiled.

As the dinner drew to a close, the head butler asked if I wanted a glass of port. 'No, thank you,' I replied. We had already enjoyed a different wine with each course, and I felt I had probably had enough. 'It really is very good port. Perfect for dessert,' he persuaded me. As the serving butler had already stepped back from the table, I watched as he was made to walk around all the other guests before arriving back to fill my glass. That no one was permitted to walk behind the Queen and the Duke was one palace protocol I watched with great curiosity. Also surprising was how warm the couple were. As we enjoyed coffee, Her Majesty spoke about her great-grandchildren just as I would about my grandchildren Allegra and Xander. We heard all about the racing car that Prince William's children played with in the garden lest they did themselves an injury indoors.

At the end of our three-and-a-half-hour lunch, I impressed upon the Queen how important it was that she return to Mansfield. She had last visited the area in 1977, the year of her silver jubilee. 'It's high time you returned. So much has changed. You will be pleased,' I said. When I briefly met her again at a celebration of the Commonwealth in 2018, I was surprised and pleased that she remembered exactly who I was. 'It's lovely to see you again, Dame Asha. How are things at the college?' she smiled as she took my hand.

While royal recognition was very gratifying, I also enjoyed two more personal achievements closer to home that meant equally as much. In May 2017, two further honours were bestowed on me. While I am not a person who naturally shows vulnerability or emotion, I was moved to tears when the business and enterprise group Mansfield 2020, which I had developed such close ties with from the outset, presented me with a lifetime achievement award. Not only did the group pay tribute to the investment I had spearheaded to transform the college, but it also heralded the opening of Mansfield's first university centre, which became a reality that year. Then, in front of 250 guests, a presentation was made by the chairman Russell Jones and by Caroline Cox, charting my journey from Bihar to Mansfield and from a child bride to a Dame. At that, I felt so overwhelmed that I felt a tear trickle down my cheek. To be recognised nationally and globally is an amazing feeling, but to know I made a real difference to the community I had put my heart and soul into was incredible.

That same month, I also took up the position of Deputy Lieutenant of Staffordshire. In this role, which I continue to this day, I help the Lord Lieutenant with his ceremonial duties throughout the year, which include representing him at civic events. My nomination for this role came from top civil servant Richard Tilbrook in recognition of my service to the local community.

By 2017, with the college numbers boosted and our new facilities opened, I started to think about my own future. For the past 10 years I, alongside dedicated staff, had taken the college from a failing institution to one that had a place on the national and international map. We had been kept on our toes from day one. We worried about students and whether they would settle in and flourish. We worried about the quality of the teaching that we were offering. And most of all, we worried about how we would cater for everyone we had set out to support, even when there were cuts in government funding. It is and remains to this day, a frustration of mine that while I was able to raise the profile of the FE sector, I was powerless to stop the constant churn of conflicting government policy, changes to the curriculum, funding changes and changes to inspection criteria, to name a few. Although I raised the problem of this short-term mindset regularly, it often fell on deaf ears. Anyone involved in the education sector will know that ministers come and go, and policy changes happen without any real analysis of the impact on the ground. Nationwide, colleges are constantly having to restructure and re-engineer to juggle ever-changing and often ill-thought-out funding demands.

Against that challenging backdrop, we built the college up to be one of the best in the country, but that also took its toll personally. There are many times during my career when all three of my children reminded me that I was not spending enough time with them. Nevertheless, when I discussed with Shankar in early 2017 that I was considering taking retirement, he persuaded me otherwise. The college was doing well, and I was still a spritely 65-year-old. 'Why stop now?' he told me. 'There's more you can do!' My board also expressed a desire for me to stay, and in the end, instead of the usual six-month notice of retirement, I started 2018 by giving the college 12 months to find my successor. By then, I would be 67, ready to hang up my gown and mortarboard.

What no one, least of all myself, had predicted was the change in government policy and in funding that would alter the landscape of the apprenticeship model so drastically. The model that West Nottinghamshire College relied so heavily upon – and that we had built much of our reputation around delivering – was no longer working. The changes focussed on the way we subcontracted our apprenticeships, and we were now set to lose millions in management fees. Many colleges around the country were facing the same financial crisis, but as we had the largest apprenticeship programme, it would affect us the most. Alongside this, we were also feeling the impact of a prolonged demographic downturn that had impacted our 16- to 18-year-old full-time student numbers and therefore our funding.

To cope with these changes, I knew that the college would have to undergo a painful restructure. In the past, we had always innovated around similar changes and came out the other side. We became magicians and succeeded. However, this was set to reduce our numbers so greatly that we realised quickly the fallout would be a lot more significant than we had planned for.

At first, we looked at the college assets, namely the e-learning business BKSB, which was profitable. However, the only potential buyer did not offer us a good deal, in my view. Certainly, in the short term, the sale would have plugged our financial shortfall, but it would not have served the college in the long term. With a heavy heart but with my board's approval, I refused it. When all other options were exhausted, I had no choice but to approach the Skills Funding Agency to ask for a £2.1m loan – a comparatively small sum compared to other colleges that had received funding over a sustained period. What I had never imagined was that this would spark an immediate intervention by the FE commissioner, Richard Atkins – a man who I knew and who I had personally supported in the past.

Meanwhile, there was a new broom at the Skills Funding Agency. The previous director there had been in post for 20 years and understood the FE sector. He appreciated its turbulence and the many challenges college principals faced, and he always took a well-considered approach to problem solving. What was heart-breaking for me personally were the significant cutbacks and redundancies we had to make. As a college, we had achieved great things together. I had nurtured many of my staff, and having to sack or move them was one of the most upsetting experiences of my life. Afterwards, those staff whose livelihoods were affected certainly thought about me and the senior team differently.

There also seemed to be a perplexing turnaround in the view of Richard Atkins. On the days he visited the college to compile his report, he reminded me, very harshly, that the college had a high-profile reputation and that I had personally built this high profile. His outbursts in every meeting about my national and international reputation left me in no doubt that his criticism was personal rather than professional. His subsequent report, due out four weeks after his visit, was leaked to the press before its official publication. Whether he was jealous of the success that I had built, I will never know, but it is the first time in my entire career that I had ever felt that being a female and being of an ethnic minority had counted against me. Normally, I would never have reached that conclusion, but I had seen other BAME colleagues attacked in similar circumstances and forced to step down. Perhaps I had been blind to a deep-seated racism. Perhaps I was also a victim of my own success.

However, by far the biggest disappointment I faced was that my chair and vice-chair on the college board who had sung my praises ahead of the commissioner's visit now turned against me to protect their own positions. Throughout my life at the college, I had created so many leaders and built an institution that was an exemplar of learning and a bedrock in the communities we served, and this felt devastating. I rang my long-term mentor Jean Hardy whose advice I had always trusted. 'Take your retirement now, Asha. Just leave,' she told me. Deep down, I knew she was right, but it did not make it easier to hear. Cutting ties with an establishment I had watched grow and prosper in such a way was agonising, but at 6 a.m. the next morning, I tendered my resignation. By stepping down, I also knew I was safeguarding the long-term future of the college. Establishments whose management are not viewed favourably, for whatever reason, are always penalised when it comes to future funding. In the end, I did not take the pay-out I was due. I had worked all my life to make a positive impact and not for money, and I did not want money now.

With hindsight, the way I exited West Nottinghamshire College was a bitter setback to me personally, but more than that, it was a blow to the sector. When principals leave in this way, any chance of them putting to good use all the experience and knowledge they have amassed over many years is greatly diminished. My ability to influence real change in the sector could have been ongoing after my retirement. Now, several years on, I realise that in the end, leadership involved me taking the personal blame for collective decisions. It is not a period I choose to dwell on, but what comforts me is that I know in my heart that I never once compromised my integrity, nor could I have done anything more.

His Royal Highness the Prince of Wales presenting the Insignia during my investiture ceremony at Buckingham Palace for my Damehood in March 2014

With my family from left to right Sneh, me, Shankar, Shalini and Sheel in the courtyard of Buckingham Palace following my investiture

In the courtyard of Buckingham Palace with the Queen's Guard just after I was made a Dame

The poster lovingly prepared by the college staff to mark my investiture celebration

With my family at the evening reception following my investiture on 14 March 2014 in London

Welcoming our guests at the evening reception

Looking amazed and overwhelmed to see so many of our friends and colleagues at the reception

Being appointed Deputy Lieutenant of Staffordshire at the ceremony by the Lord Lieutenant Ian Dudson CBE in 2017

Honoured to meet Her Majesty the Queen Elizabeth at Buckingham Palace during the Commonwealth reception in April 2018

Being interviewed by students in my office following the celebrations of achievement event at the college

West Nottinghamshire college, Derby Road campus, when I joined in 2006 as Principal and Chief Executive and the same campus following its reconstruction and transformation

Standing proud in my office at the college following completion of the renovation project

Epilogue : A New Chapter

'Go confidently in the direction of your dreams. Live the life you have imagined'

Henry David Thoreau

There is one trip to India that Shankar and I embarked on that touched us more spiritually than perhaps any other. In December 2019, we visited the historical temples of Khajuraho as well as the holy cities of Haridwar, Rishikesh and Varanasi. There, the Grand Aarti is a spiritual phenomenon that touches your soul, and we felt blessed to be able to participate in it. In Varanasi, on the banks of the River Ganges, we stood with crowds of visitors and mourners, watching the river flow and the hundreds of funeral pyres lining its banks. In the inky darkness of the night, the spit and crackle of the embers from the cremation ghats burned our eyes and hit the back of our throats. In that moment, I wondered what it is I would leave behind. How did I treat people? How did I create relationships? What did I do to make a difference in the world? In many ways, the visit brought more questions to my mind than it did answers. I realised I still had more to give.

In my retirement, I have had the pleasure of spending more time with my children and enjoying my two young grandchildren Allegra and Xander. Shankar and I have also embarked on a new chapter. That we have been married for 54 years is a constant source of amazement to both of us. From the first time I set eyes on him from the balcony in Bettiah to today, he has been my guiding force – my greatest supporter and my harshest critic – but he has always been by my side. This year, in honour of his own retirement, I wrote a special message to him:

The time is now right for a new chapter, new discoveries and for us to together live our lives to the full again... In a lifetime of togetherness, growing up together since our teens, I have learned so much about both of us. Your student days and me as young bride, your medical training and us starting our family, the joy of our youth, us often receiving compliments about our looks and sometimes being mistaken as brother and sister. Financial struggles, family pressures, at times your firm stubbornness and my naive behaviour, getting angry and coming together – all this shaped who we are today. Coming to England and learning all over again everything there was to learn, and the learning does not stop... We admire, respect and love you very much. We also take you for granted for your kindness, generosity and care. Thank you for being our rock and our inspiration. Just remember nothing has changed. It's just that you will now have more time to enjoy life the way you want it.

Where we spend our retirement will also be incredibly special. Twenty years after we began, we have created the house of our dreams from the shell of a home we bought in Rangemore, near Burton-on-Trent, all those years ago. In many ways, it reminds us of the farmhouse I had left behind in Riga when I was still a child. Surrounded by the familiar sight of cows, its beauty is one that we have never tired of. Instead of decorating it as a traditional English house, we brought a little piece of India to England and set about designing it as a Rajasthani manor house, known back home as a haveli. We had become enchanted by this style after Shankar and I took the train – The Palace on Wheels – from Delhi through India's golden triangle in Rajasthan, the state from which both our families originated. There, we travelled from the Amber Fort at Jaipur to the havelis of Jaisalmer to the ivory marble beauty of the Taj Mahal in Agra, built by the Mughal emperor Shah Jahan as the resting place for his beloved wife. We will never forget passing through its beautiful arched gateway and standing in front of the Taj Mahal taking in its wonderful landscaped gardens, leading to this most intricately carved building and minarets. Nothing could prepare us for its mystery and allure, standing with a timeless and almost regal air.

At the heart of our home, we have a beautiful kitchen. There are welcoming guest rooms and a stunning wooden-panelled staircase flanked by stained-glass windows. Shankar even has his own snooker room, this time with a full-sized table. As the house is south-facing, the light streams through, and from our windows, we can watch the sunrise and sunset over fields that stretch for miles. In winter, if we are lucky, the snow dusts the pines. In the spring and summer, the cherry blossoms flower on the trees. Finally, last year, we installed lighting along our sweeping driveway, and our project is complete. Creating our own Indian manor house has been a labour of love, but we enjoy every moment of being at home, sitting outside and enjoying the view, entertaining guests and soaking up the peace and atmosphere of rural England in our friendly little village.

I also continue with the many duties I took on while I was principal. My role as a founding trustee in the Inspire and Achieve Foundation continues. It remains as challenging as it is rewarding. In my role as Deputy Lieutenant of Staffordshire, I have the pleasure of presiding over the citizenship ceremonies of many immigrants who have made their way to the UK, just as Shankar and I did, in the hope of building a better life for themselves and for their families. 'Take all the opportunities this country offers you,' I tell them. 'You won't ever look back with regret'.

I have also been able to use my influence as a member of the Honours Committee – a post I was invited to following my damehood in 2014. There, I sat on the Education Committee for several years and also on the Diversity and Inclusion Committee. To see more people from diverse backgrounds come through the honours system and be recognised for the contribution they have made to society has been gratifying, but I also know much more needs to be done. Rewarding the top echelons of the nation is all well and good, but if we really want to make a difference, we must nurture everybody from the ground up.

My journey from child bride to damehood has been one of struggle and hardship but also one of much pleasure and fulfilment. There are also many questions I would still like to answer. How can I make a greater difference to the development of our youth? How can I enhance their skills and their development? How is it that in the 21st century young people are still being failed by our system? In our post-pandemic world, I believe this question will be more important than ever.

As our world is becoming smaller, there are more opportunities than ever to connect young people so that they can learn about the world around them and grow. When opportunity is there, they must be in a position to take it. As for myself, I will also continue to learn and grow, as I have always done. Mine is the page of learning, and a new chapter awaits…

Blessed to have the opportunity to visit the world-famous Golden Temple in Amritsar

We are admiring the spiritual settings of Ghats on the bank of the Holi River Ganga during our visit to Varanasi in December 2019

Privileged to be witnessing Ashoka Stambh in Sarnath, known to have been established in 250 BC by the Emperor Ashoka.

Our home sweet home since 1998 located in the beautiful surroundings of Needwood Forest

Our Innocent Neighbours

Winter wonders at Needwood Manor

An early evening at the Manor

Our loving children

Shalini Khemka

Shalini was an academic scholar at Moreton Hall school in Shropshire. She obtained a degree in Economics from the University of Essex. Shalini is the Founder and CEO of E2Exchange, one of the UK's leading organisations to support entrepreneurs. We are very proud and blessed that she has been appointed CBE, Commander of the Most Excellent Order of the British Empire in the Queen's New Year's Honours 2022 for her services to entrepreneurship and the economy.

Sheel Khemka

Sheel was an academic scholar at Harrow School, then he studied PPE (Politics, Philosophy, Economics) at Christchurch College, University of Oxford.

Amongst other things, Sheel is passionate about launching and establishing his fashion brand, DAgoulT.

Sneh Khemka

Sneh was also an academic scholar at Harrow school. He studied Medicine at the University of Edinburgh and qualified as an Ophthalmic Surgeon from the Royal College of Ophthalmologists in London. He has since established himself in the private healthcare sector and is currently the CEO of Simply Health, one of the UK's leaders in the provision of healthcare. Sneh has been honoured as Fellow of Public Health by Warwick University and in 2021, he was appointed an Honorary Professor of Healthcare by the University of Wales.

We feel very proud of all our three children.
We wish them all continued success and happiness.
We are honoured and humbled as a family.

To the most special mother in the world

You make us proud and happy
every single moment of every single day.

We love you very much.
Sneh, Sheel, Shalini

Acknowledgements

The process of writing my autobiography has been thoroughly fulfilling, yet quite exhausting. Going down memory lane and reliving the moments of our lives, reflecting on how and when things happened, our ups and downs, our challenges and struggles, and us staying strong together as a family has been a humbling experience.

I do not say this enough, but I want to take this opportunity to say to my children Shalini, Sheel and Sneh, 'thank you for giving us happiness and also the strength we needed. Your thoughtfulness, care and love for us is unparalleled.'

From the day I met Shankar, as we became husband and wife, he has been my guide, my rock and someone who has been on my side no matter what. I am indebted to him for the life we have been able to create together. His love and concern for me are beyond description. I know that without him, I would not be who I am today. I do not think I will really ever know how to thank him properly.

With God's grace, we have been blessed with two beautiful grandchildren, Allegra and Xander. Their love and affection touch our hearts every day, and they give me a feeling of inner contentment that is indescribable. I want to say thank you to Katarina and Sneh for giving us our precious gifts.

I believe my upbringing and my happy and confident childhood shaped me into the person I became. I pay my heartfelt tribute to my late parents, to my uncles and aunts and to my brothers Umesh, Suresh and Dinesh for everything they showered on me. My late grandmother has a special place in my heart. I am struggling to find the words, but I know her love and blessings are always with me.

I also pay my deep regards to my late mother in-law and father in-law for their graceful and nurturing love during the time I spent with them as a young bride.

I would like to express my sincere gratitude to Helena Drakakis for her help in writing my autobiography and to StoryTerrace for their support. It has been a huge pleasure to work with Helena and to get to know her.

Accolades

- Companion (CCMI), Chartered Management Institute, 2018
- Fellow, Learning and Work Institute, 2018
- Asian Businesswoman of the Year, GG2 2017
- Lifetime Achievement Award presented by 'Mansfield 2020' in 2017
- Deputy Lieutenant (DL) of Staffordshire, 2017
- Patron, Asian Apprenticeship Awards, 2016
- Woman of the Year, GG2, 2014
- Dadabhai Naoroji Award, 2014
- Dame Commander of the Most Excellent Order of the British Empire (DBE), 2014
- Inspirational Woman of the Year, East Midlands Chamber of Commerce, 2011
- Business Personality of the Year, Mansfield and Ashfield Chad Business Awards, 2011
- Winner, Non-resident Indian Awards: three categories, 2010–2011
- Officer of the Order of the British Empire (OBE), 2009
- Midlands Businesswoman of the Year, Vitalise, 2009
- Asian Woman of Achievement, Lloyds TSB, 2008
- Winner of the Jewel Award, Lloyds TSB, 2007

Letters of Compliment

24th February 2009

Dear Mrs Khemka

The Prince of Wales has asked me to write to you to express his most enormous thanks for all that you did to make his visit to the West Nottinghamshire College last Friday so interesting and enjoyable.

I know that his royal highness was greatly encouraged to meet you and your staff and students, and to see the wonderful work that you are doing there with your young people.

This comes with all best wishes.

Yours sincerely
Jonathan Hellewell
The assistant Private Secretary to TRH the Prince of Wales and the Duchy of Cornwall

19 March 2013

Dear Asha Khemka

I wanted to take a moment to write and thank you for accompanying me to India last month as I'm sure you are aware it was the largest ever UK trade delegation. I hope that you and your organisation found the trip as fruitful as we did.

We would welcome any feedback on how we can make such visits work even better for your company in the future. I enclose a CD of photographs as a Momento from the trip I hope you enjoy this as much as I have and that we have an opportunity to travel together again in the near future.

With Best wishes

David Cameron
The Prime Minister

2nd January 2014

Dear Asha

Many, many congratulations on the announcement yesterday of your honour.

This is a wonderful tribute to your personal leadership in the further education sector and, of course, a particular delight to all of us who value the great contribution of Britain's Indian community. I think you must be the first British Indian woman to become a Dame, an even greater achievement.

I look forward very much to seeing you either in London or in Delhi. In the meantime, warm congratulations and best wishes for a wonderful New Year.

Patricia Hewitt
(Former Secretary of State for Health, UK)

3 January 2014

Dear Asha

I was delighted to learn of your appointment as a Dame in the new year's honours. Your contribution to the achievement of local young people has been outstanding for so many years and you are a much-valued partner of this County. I have always enjoyed working with you, recognising that your ambition and drive is the catalyst for a step change in culture, ambition and outcomes. No matter what challenge you are presented with, your drive and determination mean that you find a way to succeed and I admire you greatly for that vision. West Nottinghamshire College has been the beneficiary of your leadership and foresight and I have no doubt that there is more to come in the New Year ahead.

I hope to continue our work together in the future. In the meantime, I want to pay tribute to your achievements and say how pleased I am that you have been recognised in this way.

Yours sincerely
Anthony May
Corporate Director
Nottinghamshire County Council

6th January 2014

Dear Dame Asha

It is very humbling to have seen the transformations that you have delivered as principal of West Nottinghamshire College and your relentless focus on getting young people into apprenticeships and jobs. I very much enjoyed my visit, your presentation and witnessing the incredible energy of the inspiring young people whom I met, in particular, the musicians.

It is the progress that you are delivering that will change the life chances of so many young people, and the leadership that you espouse that will contribute to drive up standards in the further education sector.

On behalf of the Labour Party, I want to take this opportunity to thank you for your years of service and the transformations that you have overseen; and wish you all the very best for the future.

Yours ever
Tristram Hunt MP
House of Commons

6 January 2014

Dear Asha

I was delighted to hear of you being awarded a DBE (Dame Commander of the Order of the British Empire) in the new year's honours list for services to further education.

As a result of all your hard work, commitment and dedication, Asha, which is a credit to yourself, has made the college 'outstanding', 'dynamic' and 'inspirational' in helping those students who are driven to better themselves, achieve their goals and reach new heights.

Many congratulations on such a prestigious title well deserved.

Yours sincerely
Councillor Alan Rhodes
Leader of Nottinghamshire County Council

7 January 2014

Dear Asha

It was a privilege to travel with you on the Prime Minister's delegation to India last year, where I witnessed first-hand your passion and commitment to education. Through your leadership, West Nottinghamshire College is one of the most successful colleges in Britain. You are an advocate for education and the power that it possesses to transform people's lives for the better, which is evidently seen through your charity which seeks to empower people through education not just in Britain but across the world. My heartiest congratulations on being named a Dame Commander of the order of the British Empire in the Queen's New Year's Honours list 2014. I wish you all the very best for the future and look forward to seeing you again soon in the coming year.

With kind regards

Your sincerely
Dolar
Lord Popat of Harrow
*House of Lords, Lond*on

8 January 2014

Dear Asha

Great Britain is not great because it was erstwhile ruler of an empire stretching over five continents, from Gibraltar to Hong Kong, Cape Town to Melbourne and Vancouver to San Francisco.

It is great because Britons are reasonable and considerate people. They appreciate merit if you have any; they recognise your talent without any malice regarding cast and creed. These are their virtues for which no other nation comes parallel to them. I am proud to salute the head of the nation, Her Majesty the Queen.

Yours loving uncle
Devi
Devi Prasad Agrawal

9th January 2014

Dear Dame Asha

Many congratulations on your DBE in the new year's honours list, recognising your services to further education. All those who work with you will, I'm sure, agree that this honour is richly deserved.

I hope you enjoy a wonderful day at Buckingham Palace.

With congratulations and best wishes.

Matthew Hancock MP
Minister for Skills and Enterprise
Department for Business Innovation & Skills

9th January 2014

Dear Asha

Many congratulations on being honoured as Dame Commander in the New Year's Honours.

We really want to add our thanks and appreciation for the great work you have done. Your contribution to improving the life chances of Nottinghamshire's young people and adults through further education is evidenced in the drive and energy that you have shown in leading West Nottinghamshire College. You have been truly inspirational in your approach to quality education opportunities for all.

Your Damehood is richly deserved and will be well recognised in Nottingham. Enjoy your investiture at the Palace.

Your sincerely
Councillor John Collins
Leader of Nottingham City Council

10 January 2014

Dear Asha

I'm writing to congratulate you on becoming a Dame in the New Year's Honours list. This is a remarkable accomplishment, five years after receiving your OBE for services to education. Even though I am relatively new to the further education sector, I am aware of your passion and energy for FE; spreading the benefits and elevating the profile of FE on both local and national platforms. In particular, you have ignited huge interest in FE in the communities of both Mansfield and Ashfield and ensured that West Nottinghamshire College has become synonymous with excellence in apprenticeships, leaders in employer engagement, and the place where students thrive and succeed. You have played a critical role in transforming the lives of many learners; your impact cannot be underestimated.

Once again congratulations on your achievement.

Your sincerely
Barbara Spicer
Chief Executive (interim)
Skills Funding Agency

14 February 2014

Our hearty and sincere congratulations, dear Asha, on the grand honour you have received of being made "DAME". Well done. Your achievements, hard work and talents have been recognised and rewarded at the highest level. It is indeed a source of joy and huge pride for all of us, especially the Indian communities, that one of our own has been awarded with OBE and now DBE.

Your family must be so very proud of you. Congratulations to all of you.

Love and best wishes
Rita and Radha Krishna

17 March 2014

Dear Dame Asha,

I do not know how I could ever express my thanks to all of you and to West Nottinghamshire College for the splendid and memorable event on Friday evening. All of us there came away utterly inspired!

Asha, many, many congratulations on your Damehood. What a privilege for all of us to celebrate with all of you and the West Nottinghamshire College family and community on the very day itself!

Having known you all these years, I still learnt so much more about you that evening - it is just remarkable what you have achieved. As Shankar's father said to him, 'this girl will inspire generations to come'!

I did not realise that you are the first Indian-born Dame in over eight decades – what an achievement!

With warmest regards and best wishes from Heather as well.

Karan F Bilimoria
The Lord Bilimoria, CBE, DL
House of Lords

21st March 2014

My dear Asha,

First of all, may I congratulate you again on the signal owner of the award to you in the New Year's Honours of Dame Commander of the Most Excellent Order of the British Empire. This award celebrates and rewards you for your fearless achievement in education both at West Nottinghamshire College and nationally.

I was so pleased to have been invited and it was the very greatest privilege to attend the brilliant evening last Friday when your family, friends and colleagues came together in such a splendid way to celebrate your Damehood and the investiture by Prince Charles that very morning. I will always remember the theme of the evening: family, education and hard work.

Asha, I salute you and we must keep in touch.

Yours ever
Andrew

Sir Andrew Buchanan Bt., KCVO
Lord Lieutenant (former)
Nottinghamshire

22 October 2014

Dear Asha

Many congratulations on winning the first ever Dadabhai Naoroji award.

This did not happen by accident, it reflects your tremendous achievements over the past few years in the education field. It reflects something else too; the very high esteem in which you are held, both inside the UK government, and outside – in the education world and in the UK and India more widely.

I'm delighted for you. I look forward to congratulating you in person when we next meet, either here or in the UK.

With best wishes,
James Bevan

Sir James Bevan KCMG, High Commissioner
British High Commission, New Delhi

20 January 2015

Dear Asha ji

You and Shankar are kind, caring, sincere and very dear friends. It was a great honour and immense pleasure to have you both at Sanghol. Your speech and presentation were excellent. By your caring attitude to all who had the opportunity of meeting with you, you have won their hearts and minds. They were all touched by your kind and caring manner. The feedback of your visit is unmatched by any of the previous visitors to the campus over the last many years.

They will be eagerly waiting for your next visit. Warm regards and very best wishes.

Diljit
Lord Rana MBE, Baron of Malone

4 June 2015

Dear Dame Asha Khemka

Thank you for arranging an instructive and pleasant programme for my visit to the West Nottinghamshire College group. I was very pleased to have the opportunity to see the various skill development Institutes within the college group and was greatly impressed by the enormous contribution you have made personally to the development of a world-class institution. Your achievements are certainly a matter of pride for us.

I was also honoured to see so many distinguished leaders of the local community over the informal lunch which you had arranged. We would like to continue to build strong relationships in all parts of the UK and such interactions are most useful.

I do hope that in the future there would be possibilities for building collaborations with institutions in India working on skills development. I look forward to staying in touch.

Your sincerely
Ranjan Mathai
*High Commiss*ioner of India to the UK

6 January 2016

Dear Asha

We were delighted to launch the Midlands engine for growth initiative with you to promote the region as a hub for innovation and manufacturing with Indian education, business and industry partners. Your commitment and enthusiasm have helped make this visit a great success in broadcasting our positive message about welcoming India's brightest and the best students to our world-class universities.

We are keen to continue to work closely with you on this fast moving and ambitious agenda over the coming year and look forward to welcoming you on future engagements in India soon.

Thank you again for your participation and valued contribution.

Yours sincerely,

Sajid Javid MP
Secretary of State for Business, Innovation and Skills

Jo Johnson MP
Minister for Universities

19 October 2018

Dear Asha

I wanted to write on behalf of myself and my board colleagues to thank you for all your hard work on the Institute for Apprenticeships board.

You were an outstanding candidate and I was delighted when the Secretary of State appointed you to the board. Your knowledge of the sector and passion for apprenticeships and technical education is unmatched and we benefited greatly from it. The mission of the Institute is complex and difficult and yet you embraced it with energy, wisdom and great leadership. This was also true of your work on the Quality Assurance Committee.

We were all very fortunate to have you as a colleague and you will be greatly missed.

I wish you all the very best for the future and please do stay in touch.

Kind regards

Antony Jenkins
Chairman
Institute for Apprenticeships

Blessings From My Dear Uncle

I had an opportunity to join Asha at the launch celebrations of AoC India at the British High Commission in New Delhi on 22 January, 2013. Asha was leading a team of educationalists from the United Kingdom. While in conversation with Ms Susan Pember, a senior British education official, I said, 'My family and our country are grateful to your nation for bestowing Asha with both opportunity and honour.' Her reply was, 'Mr Agrawal, Britain is grateful to your family and your country for giving us Asha Khemka, who is our Queen of Education.'

The statement, even today, reflects multiple shades of meaning: Great Britain embraces talent and quality with gratitude, and for this nation a person's contribution and the two nations' mutual relations are more important than mere citizenship of the country. Today, I am very proud of both Asha and the United Kingdom.

India's traditional teaching is the creation of great teachers and we feel honoured to see Asha, daughter of Bihar, carry forward the legacy of the land enlightened by visionaries like Gautama Buddha and Kautilya (Chanakya).

Immense love and blessings to you, Asha!

When we think of Asha's achievements as an educationalist in a land thousands of miles away from her own native land, the impossible became inevitable; and this has been possible because of her determination, dedication and discipline.

I wish her all the glory and success and congratulate her for bringing in her experience in the form of this book.

I am confident this book will underscore the integral and eternal relationship of education and educationalist and will inspire the generations to come.

Ram Sharan Agrawal

My recent duties in my role as Deputy Lieutenant of Staffordshire

I was honoured to light up the Beacon at Lichfield Cathedral to celebrate the Platinum Jubilee of Queen Elizabeth II on 2nd June 2022

My tribute to Her Majesty the late Queen as aired on ITV Central News in Great Britain on 13th September 2022

"Dame who met the Queen on many occasions will travel to London to pay her respects"

Asha Khemka has been reflecting on her interactions with The Queen and what Her Majesty meant to her.

Dame and Deputy Lieutenant of Staffordshire, Asha Khemka, is one of the many Midlands residents who are travelling to London to pay their respects to the Queen this week.

Mrs Khemka, who lives in Burton-upon-Trent, received an OBE from the Queen in 2009. She said she has felt honoured to have a number of interactions with the Queen.

The OBE recipient was also made a Dame in 2014 by the UK's longest reigning monarch.

Speaking to ITV News Central, Mrs Khemka said: "The first time when I met her it was during my OBE. Receiving this kind of honour from the Queen of the United Kingdom - it means something."

"She looked just like a mother figure to me. The way she was warm and holding my hand and talking to me."

Dame Asha recalls being admired for the sari she was wearing at the Queen's Diwali party.

"She spoke to me and looked into my eyes and we were talking just like we had known each other for a very, very long time. I was invited on 2 or 3 occasions to Buckingham Palace."

"One was the Diwali party and we had a fantastic time and I was admired for the sari that I was wearing for that. I was also invited for a private lunch with Her Majesty."

"I took as a gift for her, a miners lamp from Mansfield - the mining area - and she says 'Dame Asha, you have brought the most appropriate gift from Mansfield.' and I said to Her Majesty. 'Your Majesty please don't call me Dame Asha, I'm Asha.'

“She said, ‘We have made you a Dame, we'd better call you a Dame.’

“All of those mixed feelings in my heart, of knowing her, meeting her, talking to her, celebrating her, celebrating her reign over those many years, and then all of a sudden, she is no more.”

“It was my honour, privilege to announce about the proclamation and about the passing of Her Majesty the Queen. The way she did her job, not just in this country but the world over. She is the Queen.”

“She is the Queen of the world, not just the United Kingdom.”

It was my privilege to lead the Proclamation Ceremony of King Charles III

On Saturday 10 September, 2022, the new sovereign was proclaimed. Across the nations, ceremonies took place to proclaim King Charles III as the new King of Great Britain.

In Tamworth, the Proclamation took place at the Town Hall, Market Street on Sunday 11 September, 2022, at 2.30pm. This official Proclamation for the new Monarch was read out by the Deputy Lord Lieutenant of Staffordshire, Dame Asha Khemka DBE, and Tamworth's Mayor.

Crowds gathered for this historic occasion. Staffordshire Deputy Lieutenant Dame Asha Khemka DBE said: "We come together this afternoon following the passing of our late Sovereign, Queen Elizabeth the Second. Our sadness at this time is shared by people across the globe, as we remember with affection and gratitude the lifetime of service given by our longest-reigning Monarch.

"But the basis on which our monarchy is built has ensured that through the centuries the Crown has passed in an unbroken line of succession. Today's ceremony marks the formal Proclamation to the people of Staffordshire the beginning of our new King's reign."

AND THE STORY CONTINUES ....